Robert Burns

Ian Grimble

HAMLYN

First published 1986 by Hamlyn Publishing
Bridge House, London Road, Twickenham, Middlesex

© Copyright Ian Grimble 1986

ISBN 0 600 50123 X

Printed in Portugal

Foreword

I WOULD LIKE to express my gratitude to William Carrocher, brought up in the farming country of Ayrshire and educated at Ayr Academy, for the helpful advice he has given to me. He is the only living Scot of my acquaintance equally fluent in the language of Burns and in the Gaelic language which was still spoken from one end of Greenock High Street to the other long after the bard's death. Consequently it was likely to have infiltrated the Scots speech of Ayrshire, and Carrocher was able to tell me of surviving idioms that show this to have been the case.

I owe a second debt of gratitude to Andrew, Earl of Elgin and Kincardine for the valuable information he has given me about Freemasonry in Scotland, and also for placing some of his family papers at my disposal. The use I have made of his help will appear in the text.

Those interested in discovering how the Scots language in its modern, standardized form is used today as a vehicle for literature should consult *Lallans: The Magazine for Writing in Lowland Scots*. Number 14, published in 1980, contains Donald Campbell's vigorous translation of Rob Donn Mackay's Gaelic Poem on *The Misers*. It may be compared with the vernacular as Burns used it in the 18th century, and provoke reflections on what might have been if the Ayrshire bard had enjoyed the same access to the compositions of his literary twin.

Contents

Introduction

ROBERT BURNS is one of the most fascinating human beings on record. Today the world knows it, and in his own lifetime many of his acquaintances expressed their awareness of it. Of these, none left a more graphic description of that magnetic presence than Maria Riddell, the last and most intelligent woman with whom he formed a friendship.

'His features were stamped with the hardy character of independence, and the firmness of conscious, though not arrogant, pre-eminence; the animated expressions

The poet James Montgomery (1771–1854). Though born in Irvine, he was of Irish parentage and returned to Ireland during his childhood. His comment on the language of Burns's poetry must be considered in this light.

of countenance were almost peculiar to himself; the rapid lightnings of his eye were always the harbingers of some flash of genius, whether they darted the fiery glances of insulted and indignant superiority, or beamed with the impassioned sentiment of fervent and impetuous affections. His voice alone could improve upon the magic of his eye; sonorous, replete with the finest modulations, it alternately captivated the ear with the melody of poetic numbers, the perspicuity of nervous reasoning, or the ardent sallies of enthusiastic patriotism.' It sounds almost too good to be true, but others – and they were men – said much the same.

Mrs Riddell, who was not star-struck, described another aspect of the bard's many-sided personality. 'The keenness of satire was, I am almost at a loss whether to say his forte or his foible; for though nature had endowed him with a portion of the most pointed excellence in that dangerous talent, he suffered it too often to be the vehicle of personal, and sometimes unfounded, animosities. It was not always that sportiveness of humour, that "unwary pleasantry", which Sterne has depicted with touches so conciliatory, but the darts of ridicule were frequently directed as the caprice of the instant suggested, or as the altercations of parties and of persons happened to kindle the restlessness of his spirit into interest or aversion.' All the peculiarities of this complicated man, which Maria Riddell described within a few days of his death, can be seen in his writings, as well as in his life.

In the case of his writings it is not only what he said, but the language in which he said it, that has been a subject of endless analysis, much of it contradictory. For instance in 1809 one Scot, Francis Jeffrey, said of the language of his dialect poetry, 'It is the language of a whole country . . . the common speech of the whole nation in early life.' As a matter of incontrovertible fact it was totally unintelligible in the Gaelic-speaking half of Scotland, while Wordsworth remarked that he could understand it without difficulty because it resembled his local English dialect. To complicate matters

Francis Jeffrey (1773–1850). Literary critic, editor of the influential Edinburgh Review, *and an advocate who was raised to the judicial bench as Lord Jeffrey, he asserted that Scots was 'the common speech of the whole nation in early life'. Engraving, 1847, by G. Parker from a portrait by Colvin Smith.*

further, another Scot, James Montgomery, asserted, also in 1809: 'there is not a poem of Burns (the *mere*, not *pure*, English ones excepted) composed in a dialect spoken by any class of men in our whole island.'

What Burns achieved in the language he chose to use can be understood best by glancing at the linguistic situation in Scotland in his time. In slightly more than half the area of the country Gaelic was spoken, and the majority of those who used it understood no English. Gaelic was the original language of the Scots, brought by them from Ireland (where they had been known as *Scotti*) when they first colonized western Scotland at the end of the 5th century. This language had the oldest literature in Europe after those of Greek and Latin, and most of the best Scottish poets when Burns was born were still Gaelic ones. These included the most distinguished of all, the Jacobite Alexander Mac-Donald, whose poetry was published in Edinburgh in 1751. Dugald Buchanan was the outstanding religious poet of this time, whose Gaelic poetry appeared in print in Edinburgh in 1767. Gaelic had been the earliest language in Europe in which nature was celebrated, and this tradition produced Scotland's greatest nature poet in Duncan Macintyre from Glenorchy, who came to Edinburgh in 1767 to take employment in the city guard and spent half his lifetime in the capital. Here the first edition of his Gaelic poetry was published in 1768 while Burns was a child, the second in 1790 when the poet from Ayrshire had outstripped him in celebrity.

Although Burns, in common with most Lowlanders, never attempted to learn the original language of the Scots, he grew up in the same country as these other poets and was moved by the same influences. He composed Jacobite verse like MacDonald and nature poetry like Macintyre. But there was another bard, forty-five years old when Burns was born, named Robert Mackay and generally known as Rob Donn, who was so similar to Robert Burns in his attitudes and utterances that they seem to have been created in the same mould, as indeed they were. Rob Donn lived in Sutherland in the far north and understood no English, and it is most singular that the spirit of an age could produce two singers who shared no common language and yet who sang so nearly in the same voice. This phenomenon hints at mysterious forces, underlying the more obvious ones, which delivered Robert Burns to the world.

As for the linguistic heritage at his own disposal, it was based on the English language that had flooded into southern Scotland in the wake of the Saxon Queen, Saint Margaret, wife of Malcolm Canmore, after the Norman conquest of England in 1066. In the southern kingdom French became the language of the court and administration for the next 400 years. But many of the Anglo-Saxon aristocracy found an asylum at the Scottish court, from where their language spread to the towns and became the language of commerce as well as the vehicle for a distinguished literature. The 15th century Stewart King James I composed a fine poem in English, when it was inconceivable that a Plantagenet would have done the same. The same century witnessed the compositions of such excellent poets as Henryson and Dunbar in Scotland during an age of silence in England after the death of Chaucer in 1400.

When this silence was broken by the Elizabethan poets, the language had altered radically during the interval. In Scotland by contrast, the literary continuity had helped to preserve an older form of English, as we can see in Sir David Lindsay's *Satire of the Three Estates*, composed in the age of the Tudor poets. Based on northern Middle English in the first place, this language came to be known as the old Scots tongue. It suffered an eclipse in the 17th century when the language of letters in Scotland moved towards conformity with that of England, its country of origin. But in rural areas, from Kent to Shetland, local dialects flourished in all their rich variety, just as Gaelic ones did, from the south of Ireland to the Butt of Lewis. In the case of the Scots ones, as the English ones in Scotland were defined, those of Shetland were deeply impregnated with the old Norse tongue while the Ayrshire dialect as naturally contained Gaelicisms.

After the incorporating Union with England of 1707 there was something of a crisis of cultural identity in Scotland, and it expressed itself in a self-conscious attitude to language. While standard English continued to be the language of prose, there were those who sought to revive the old Scots tongue as the vehicle of poetry. Gaelic poetry had flourished for centuries but the language was unknown to many, and of course Scots had never been lost in the folk songs of the countryside. But now this idiom became a vogue in fashionable drawing rooms. Aristocratic ladies composed poems in Scots, although that arbiter of literary taste in Edinburgh, the poet Dr Blacklock, who was the son of a brick-layer from Annan, would have none of this and wrote only in English. The choice had nothing to do with class, as has been suggested so often.

Before the birth of Burns there had been Elizabeth Wardlaw, daughter of a knight, wife of a baronet, to whom Percy ascribed the authorship of the ballad of Sir Patrick Spens in the bard's lifetime. In Edinburgh he met Mrs Allison Cockburn, author of the much-loved song *Flowers of the Forest*, while Mrs Cockburn's friend Lady Anne Barnard composed the equally famous *Auld Robin Gray*. When Burns first entered the lists he was imitating genteel ladies who were already writing in the Scottish folk tradition.

As for the language they spoke, Lord Cockburn the judge wrote in 1844 that 'Scotch has ceased to be the vernacular language of the upper classes.' It is doubtful whether this was wholly true. Sir Ewan Forbes, 11th Baronet of Craigievar, wrote in his book *The Aul' Days*, published in 1984, about the attitude of a north-east family of royal descent and broad acres. He related

Lady Anne Barnard (1750–1825), daughter of the 5th Earl of Balcarres. She composed 'Auld Robin Gray' at the age of 22, before spending years of her life at the Cape of Good Hope and the remainder in London. Drawing by Walter E. Cockerell.

that his own father had been 'very particular about proper Scottish upbringing as taught by his father, with an insistence on being able to speak, read and write Doric so that Scottish literature and verse could be fully enjoyed, and having a close understanding with all true residents of the land'. In saying this, Sir Ewen is describing the period of which Lord Cockburn was writing. He is also speaking of the part of the country in which the ancestors of Burns had lived for generations before his father emigrated to Ayrshire.

But he would not have found the speech of Ayrshire the same as the Doric of Aberdeenshire, while the English dialect of Shetland was more different still. There had been as yet no systematic attempt to create a standardized Scots language, and the language of the administration and most of the literature of this age

was English. In the Gaelic half of Scotland the situation was the same except that here there was no equivalent of standard English. The speech and poetry of Rob Donn were at least as different from those of Alexander MacDonald as Doric from the dialect of Ayrshire. The publication of a Gaelic New Testament in the modern vernacular in 1767 and of a Gaelic–English dictionary in 1780 did not suffice to remedy this.

Robert Burns fell heir to this situation, and it accounts for the spectrum of language he used with such art. As for what is missing from it, he was disinherited by the refusal of the Edinburgh cultural establishment to have anything to do with the rich Gaelic literary heritage on its doorstep. This provoked a Gael named James MacPherson to perpetrate one of

Above: James MacPherson (1736–1796). Author of the 'Ossianic' epics, one of the most spectacular hoaxes in the history of European literature. Engraving by C. Knight from the portrait by Sir Joshua Reynolds.

Above right: Henry Mackenzie (1745–1831). An attorney whose first novel, The Man of Feeling, *Robert Burns read in his youth and described as 'a book I prize next to the Bible'. From the portrait by William Stavely. Scottish National Portrait Gallery, Edinburgh.*

The simple Bard, rough at the rustic plough,
Learning his tuneful trade from ev'ry bough;
The chanting linnet, or the mellow thrush,
Hailing the setting sun, sweet, in the green thorn
  bush,
The soaring lark, the perching red-breast shrill,
Or deep-toned plovers, grey, wild-whistling o'er
  the hill;
Shall he, nursed in the Peasant's lowly shed,
To hardy Independence bravely bred,
By early Poverty to hardship steel'd . . . etc.
The Brigs of Ayr, a Poem.

the most spectacular frauds in the history of European letters. In 1760 he began the publication of his bogus Ossianic epics, claiming that they were English translations from Gaelic originals of immemorial antiquity. They became celebrated throughout Europe, the defence of their authenticity a patriotic duty. A Gaelic scholar in the isle of Arran named William Shaw who attempted to expose the fraud was persecuted until he was driven to take refuge in England. Burns was brought up on this rubbish and admired it deeply. Unfortunately it was to be his sole contact with the Gaelic heritage.

But he hoaxed the Edinburgh establishment in his turn. Those who sought the National Identity in the Scots tongue not unnaturally expected to find it in the humble homes of the peasantry, uncorrupted by anglicizing influences. Burns descended from a long line of tenant farmers and was at least as well educated as the average member of the gentry in his day, but he represented himself in his first published collection of poems as a mere country yokel, and the ruse succeeded.

'With what uncommon penetration and sagacity,' extolled that prince of Edinburgh critics, Henry Mackenzie, 'this Heaven-taught ploughman, from his humble and unlettered station, has looked upon men and manners'. However, he could not fool everybody, any more than James MacPherson could with his bogus Ossian. 'I received three letters from Edinburgh,' John Logan wrote to Mackenzie, 'full of irrational and unbounded panegyric, representing him as a poetical phenomenon that owed nothing but to Nature and his own Genius. When I opened the book I found that he was as well acquainted with the English poets as I was.'

A consummate actor, Robert Burns adopted many roles, matched by the range of language in which he expressed himself. In both respects he was fashioned by the characteristics of the society over which he cast such a magic spell.

Chapter 1

KINCARDINESHIRE is a little county of great beauty, enclosed by its larger neighbours, Aberdeenshire to the north and Angus to the south. Much of its northern boundary is defined by the river Dee, though it leaps these waters to enclose the lands that surround the town of Banchory on Deeside. The southern boundary is marked partly by the North Esk; and the lands between, known as the Mearns, present a vivid contrast of green growth and the rich soil of Old Red Sandstone. This was the world in which a long line of tenant farmers of the name of Burness made their living, at least from the time of William, who died in 1670.

The fertile fields of the Mearns form a plateau ending in rugged cliffs, save for the occasional creek or bay in which fishermen built their hamlets. Of these, Cattaline in particular was to inspire some of the finest paintings of Joan Eardley.

Stonehaven was the sole substantial port of Kincardineshire, close to the great castle of Dunnottar

Stonehaven, principal port of Kincardineshire. From Allan Cunningham: Pictures and Portraits of the Life and Land of Robert Burns, *1840.*

on its rock promontory above the North Sea, seat of the Earls Marischal. After the 1715 uprising in which the last Earl Marischal joined the Jacobites, Dunnottar was dismantled and remains a ruin to this day, though his red stone warehouse beside the harbour of Stonehaven has been restored as a museum. Robert Burness, grandfather of the bard, had been employed in the gardens of Dunnottar, but after the downfall of its proprietor he took a lease of the farm of Clochanhill, where his son William was born in 1721.

In the days before agricultural improvement, the Mearns could not have presented such a prosperous appearance as they do today. On the other hand, there were plenty of farmers whose labours were crowned with success, and who contributed to the gradual transformation of rural Scotland. The Burness family were not among these. They suffered a run of bad luck, generation after generation, particularly in the matter of their tenancy agreements; which leaves an impression of hereditary ineptitude. Farming was in their blood, without question, but not in their heads. The farm of Clochanhill failed: Robert Burness obtained a loan from the Provost of Aberdeen with which he added two adjacent farms to his property: the second Jacobite uprising of 1745 either did or did not ruin his second venture (there is invariably an external cause to account for the recurrent disasters): by 1748 Robert Burness had nothing to support him but the charity of his sons.

Dunnottar Castle on the coast of Kincardineshire, former seat of the Earls Marischal. From Francis Grose: The Antiquities of Scotland, *1797.*

Ayr, from Brown Carrick hill. Engraving by D. O. Hill in The Land of Burns *by Professor Wilson and Robert Chambers, 1840.*

The 'Wallace Tower', Ayr. The present one dates from 1834 and replaced an old baronial building. It is not known how the structure acquired its name though Wallace and his men burned the quarters of the English soldiers at the Barns of Ayr in the 13th century. The old tower is mentioned by Burns in The Brigs of Ayr. *From Allan Cunningham:* Pictures and Portraits of the Life and Land of Robert Burns, 1840.

through a variety of difficulties'. He migrated to Ayrshire, where he obtained a holding of seven and a half acres at Alloway near to the county town, and on it he built a two-roomed cottage of clay and thatch. William Burness was thirty-six years old by now, and he appears to have put up his house in a hurry with the intention of marrying at last. His bride, twelve years younger than himself, was Agnes Broun, daughter of a tenant farmer in the neighbourhood. In their new home she gave birth to their first son Robert on 25 January 1759.

It almost collapsed about their ears in a storm, as his brother Gilbert was to relate. 'One very stormy morning, when my brother was nine or ten days old, a little before daylight, a part of the gable fell out, and the rest appeared so shattered that my mother, with the young poet, had to be carried through the storm to a neighbour's house, where they remained a week, till their own dwelling was adjusted.' It appears to have needed something less perfunctory than a week's worth of 'adjustment', and it was indeed rebuilt in a far more substantial manner. The bard's first home was rebuilt in facsimile in 1881, and is preserved today as a museum, its walls gleaming white, its thatch in perfect condition, its rooms embellished with Burns manuscripts and other mementoes. The structure is typical of the single-storey longhouses, such as even members of the gentry inhabited in many areas of Scotland at this time. The Gaelic bard Rob Donn described just such a dwelling, after he had been taken as a herd-boy into the household of a Mackay tacksman who could matriculate a coat-of-arms, and who spent a prosperous lifetime conducting the cattle trade between Sutherland and the fairs of Crieff.

In those cosy rooms of his home in Alloway, with

The infant Robert being carried to safety by his mother on the night of the storm. Chalk drawing by Samuel Edmonston, 1897.

They scattered in all directions, as the future bard's brother Gilbert was to recall, 'each going off his several way in search of adventures, and scarcely knowing whither he went. My father undertook to act as gardener and shaped his course to Edinburgh, where he wrought hard when he could get work, passing

The room in which Burns was born. Engraving from
The Illustrated London News, *celebrating the Burns Centenary, 1859.*

Agnes Burness, née Broun (1723–1820), mother of the bard.
Anonymous portrait in a private collection.

their thick walls and little windows, young Robert first heard the folk-songs of his country from the tuneful voice of his mother. Agnes Broun was able to read the Bible but she was not able to write, and imperfect literacy has often been the best preservative of oral tradition. To supplement her own repertoire, Mrs Burness had at her elbow an elderly widowed relative named Betty Davidson, a regular visitor who aided her in her domestic work. Robert seems to have forgotten her status later, in describing her as a 'maid', when she was neither a spinster nor quite a servant. But he remembered what was important about her.

'In my infant and boyish days I owed much to an old maid of my mother's, remarkable for her ignorance, credulity and superstition. She had, I suppose, the largest collection in the county of tales and songs concerning devils, ghosts, fairies, brownies, witches, warlocks, spunkies, kelpies, elf-candles, dead-lights, wraiths, apparitions, cantraips, giants, enchanted towers, dragons and other trumpery. This cultivated the latent seeds of Poesy.'

What his sternly religious, intellectual father thought of all this we are left to guess. He composed a *Manual of Religious Belief* in which the child questions his parent, an arrangement that suggests an altogether exceptional breadth of mind. It was more usual at this time for the young to learn religious dogma by rote. Perhaps he decided that by sharpening the critical faculties of his children, he would enable them to contend with warlocks and dragons for themselves. Three more of them were born to him in his Alloway home, first Gilbert, then two daughters.

It was possible that William Burness might have added the traditions of his own native district to the household store, but this would have been a great deal to expect of a man so literate and so devout. As early as 1567, the first published Gaelic manual of Calvinist belief had warned the faithful against profane, mendacious tales and carnal music, and this attitude has continued into the 20th century. In north-east Scotland, however, there were pockets of Papists and large areas corrupted by the heresies of the Episcopal

Church, which turned a blind eye to the snares of secular song and story. One man even wrote down the music of the Irishman Rory O Cathain in the Straloch manuscript without setting fire to the paper, though the devout may note with satisfaction that this document has disappeared. Robert Burns was to set his verses, *Ae Fond Kiss* to an air it contained, calling it Rory Dall's Port, that is, Blind Rory O Cathain's Tune.

Had William Burness been in a position to marry at a more usual time of life, his son Robert might have had a mother able to impart to him the rich cultural heritage of north-east Scotland, largely enshrined in the local speech known as Doric. The themes of its songs and ballads date back to such far-off events as the battle of Harlaw in 1411, and their modern exponents have contributed a copious collection to the sound archives of the School of Scottish Studies. Distinguished modern poetry is still published in Doric. Robert Burns did well enough as a child in absorbing the folklore of Ayrshire from Agnes Broun and Betty Davidson. He would explore the Doric heritage later, assisted by the fact that so many of his Burness relatives remained in the country from which his father had emigrated.

Halloween. The 31st of October, All Hallows Eve, was the night in which ghosts and witches were most likely to be out and about. Burns heard much about them from Betty Davidson. Chalk drawing by Samuel Edmonston, 1897.

The poet's birthplace in Alloway, Ayrshire, as it was reconstructed in 1881. Scottish Tourist Board.

But from William himself the future poet received altogether different fare. A formal education of the conventional sort was what William desired for his children. Robert was sent on the mile-long journey to the little school of Alloway from the age of six, his younger brother Gilbert trotting beside him, and when the local teacher left to take up a better post, it was William Burness among all the parents of the neighbourhood who travelled to Ayr to seek a replacement for him. He interviewed a serious, pedantic youth named John Murdoch, and approved what he saw, as Murdoch himself related.

'I was engaged by Mr Burness and four of his neighbours to teach, and accordingly began to teach the little school at Alloway.' The method of payment is interesting. 'My five employers undertook to board me by turns, and to make up a certain salary at the end of the year, provided my quarterly payments from the different pupils did not amount to that sum.'

Very different from the world of brownies and giants was the one that Murdoch inhabited, and it took little Robert a while to discover any enchanted towers in it.

'My pupil Robert Burns was then between six and seven years of age; his preceptor about eighteen. Robert and his younger brother Gilbert had been grounded a little in English before they were put under my care. They both made a rapid progress in reading, and a tolerable progress in writing . . . Robert and Gilbert were generally at the upper end of the class, even when ranged with boys by far their seniors. The books most commonly used in the school were the "Spelling Book," the New Testament, the Bible, Masson's *Collection of Prose and Verse*, and Fisher's *English Grammar*.'

It says a great deal for Murdoch's integrity, writing after Robert's talents had become common knowledge, that he should have confessed his failure to recognize them in the child. 'Gilbert always appeared to me to possess a more lively imagination, and to be more of a wit than Robert. I attempted to teach them a little church music. Here they were left behind by all the rest of the school. Robert's ear, in particular, was remarkably dull, and his voice untunable. It was long before I could get them to distinguish one tune from another.' Murdoch appears to have been a conscientious and able teacher, but evidently he did not possess the key to Robert's imagination as Betty Davidson did.

But Murdoch gave him access to the printed word,

and it sufficed. 'The two first books I ever read in private, and which gave me more pleasure than any two books I ever read again, were *The Life of Hannibal* and *The History of Sir William Wallace*. Hannibal gave my young ideas such a turn that I used to strut in raptures up and down after the recruiting drum and bagpipe, and wish myself tall enough that I might be a soldier; while the story of Wallace poured a Scottish prejudice into my veins which will boil along there till the flood-gates of life shut in eternal rest.'

In Masson's *Collection* was the work of a poet from the Border country who had died only just over ten years before Robert was born. The son of a clergyman, James Thomson was sent to Edinburgh university for his education, from where he went to seek his fortune in London. In 1726 he published the first of the four poems which were collected together as *The Seasons*. In the southern capital he enjoyed the necessary patronage to live as a successful poet until his untimely death at the age of 48. He was honoured with an impressive memorial in the Poets' Corner of Westminster Abbey, and is perhaps remembered best today as the author of 'Rule Britannia'.

In his own time, *The Seasons* not only heralded the Romantic Movement in poetry: it leapt over the language barrier in Scotland. The Jacobite bard Alexander MacDonald, born at about the same time as Thomson and outliving him by decades, was inspired to compose his own poems on the seasons in Gaelic. These, passing by word of mouth to the far north of Scotland, moved Rob Donn to emulate both of them in his poem on winter. Like Robert Burns, Rob Donn was one of mid-winter's children.

> I was born in the winter
> Among the lowering mountains,
> And my first sight of the world
> Snow and wind about my ears.
> *Translation by Ian Grimble.*

The other Rob could say almost precisely the same of his own birth forty-five years later, when he wrote:

> Our monarch's hindmost year but ane
> Was five and twenty days begun,
> 'Twas then a blast o' Janwar' Win'
> Blew [hansel] in on Robin.   [the first gift]
> *There was a lad was born in Kyle*, to
> the tune *Daintie Davie*.

Both, in their rural surroundings, had their appreciation of the natural world heightened at an early age by the same influence. Burns also had before him the example of a lad of parts from the Scottish Lowlands who had not failed to find patrons as a man of letters.

While the two brothers spent two years attending the little school at Alloway, their father was making a living as a market gardener. He also acted as gardener to Dr William Fergusson, the Provost of Ayr, and however modest his circumstances William Burness would have done well to cling to what he had for fear of

finding worse. But like his father before him he determined to exchange his occupation as a gardener for the status of tenant farmer, with equally catastrophic results. In 1765 he offered to lease from Provost Fergusson a seventy-acre farm two miles from Alloway called Mount Oliphant. The terms appeared attractive, a twelve-year tenancy that might be terminated after six, and an advance of £300 from Dr Fergusson to enable William Burness to stock his farm. The family moved in the spring of 1766, and Robert and Gilbert continued to attend the school at Alloway for another two years, despite the far longer walk. Then their attendance became less regular until Murdoch left to take up another appointment and the school closed.

At Mount Oliphant the spectre of failure began to haunt the family. William Burness had evidently neglected to assess what his son Gilbert described as 'almost the very poorest soil I know of in a state of cultivation'. No longer young, nor in good health, he had not estimated the number of labourers he would require to improve such land. It was his sons who bore the brunt of his mistake. During the period of adolescence when an adequate diet is most necessary, they taxed their growing frames on the poorest of food, as Gilbert recalled. 'We lived very sparingly. For several years butcher's meat was a stranger in the house, while all members of the family exerted themselves to the utmost of their strength, and rather beyond it, in the labours of the farm. My brother at the age of thirteen assisted in threshing the crop of corn, and at fifteen was the principal labourer on the farm, for we had no hired servant, male or female. The anguish of mind we felt at our tender years, under these straits and difficulties, was very great.'

Had the boys been genuine farm servants, there would have been a limit to the work that could have been expected of them, and a minimum diet that they could have demanded. As it was, the strain imposed on Robert's heart during these years at Mount Oliphant brought on the fatal disease called endocarditis. In his

Ploughing. An early 19th-century sketch by E. A. Walton. National Galleries of Scotland, Department of Prints and Drawings.

determination to be a tenant farmer like his fathers before him, William Burness killed Scotland's greatest poet in his prime.

But no one was aware at the time that this was so, nor indeed for long after the poet's death, since his ailment was not diagnosed correctly until the present century. It was the father's health that caused the greatest concern in that isolated, tight-knit community on Mount Oliphant, increased by now to a family of seven children. 'My father,' wrote Gilbert, 'was for some time almost the only companion we had. He conversed familiarly on all subjects with us as if we had been men, and was at great pains while we accompanied him in the labours of the farm, to lead the conversation to such subjects as might tend to increase our knowledge, or confirm us in virtuous habits.' The poor lads could hardly have had much energy or opportunity to develop any vicious ones.

When he was fourteen, Robert found himself working at the harvest beside a girl of his own age named Nelly Kirkpatrick, and long remembered wondering, in his innocence, 'why my pulse beat such a furious ratann when I looked and fingered over her hand, to pick out the nettle-stings and thistles. Among her other love-inspiring qualifications, she sung sweetly; and 'twas her favourite reel to which I attempted giving an embodied vehicle in rhyme'. His father's precepts do not appear to have been put out of mind in these, Robert's earliest surviving verses.

> A bonny lass I will confess
> Is pleasant to the e'e,
> But without some better qualities
> She's no a lass for me.
>
> But Nelly's looks are blythe and sweet,
> And what is best of a',
> Her reputation is compleat,
> And fair without a flaw.
>
> *O once I lov'd.*

The farm buildings of Mount Oliphant. From Robert Fitzhugh: Robert Burns, the Man and the Poet, 1970.

Kirkoswald near Turnberry, where Burns stayed on the farm of his uncle Samuel Broun while he studied mathematics. Tam's grave is in the background. Engraving by D. O. Hill for Wilson and Chambers: The Land of Burns, *1840.*

Shanter Farm near the coast between Turnberry and Culzean, a favourite resort of smugglers. Burns recalled: 'The contraband trade was at that time very successful; scenes of swaggering riot and roaring dissipation were as yet new to me.' The sixteen year old boy's memories of Kirkoswald bore fruit in Tam o' Shanter. *Engraving by D. O. Hill for Wilson and Chambers:* The Land of Burns, *1840.*

'Thus,' Robert recalled, 'with me began Love and Poesy; which at times have been my only, and till within this last twelve-month have been my highest enjoyment.' He was writing fourteen years later, when, for the first time, he could enjoy the novel pleasure of touring his native land.

But in the year 1773 in which Nelly awoke in Robert Burns the first stirrings of love, his father once again provided a different kind of stimulus. His former teacher John Murdoch had joined the staff of the burgh school of Ayr, where William Burness arranged that his son should spend three weeks under his instruction. 'Robert Burns came to board and lodge with me, for the purpose of revising English grammar etc, that he might be better qualified to instruct his brothers and sisters at home. He was now with me day and night, in school, at all meals, and in all my walks.' The 'etc' included a short course in French which enabled Burns later, with the aid of a dictionary, to scatter French words and expressions in his letters. There were more well-to-do boys at the school, who provided, briefly, the kind of companionship in which he found so much

enjoyment all his life, and who were able to lend him books.

This respite must have made the drudgery and loneliness of Mount Oliphant all the more depressing by contrast, especially after Provost Fergusson died and his estate was managed by a harsh factor. Under the tenancy agreement, William Burness might have terminated the lease after six years, yet he did not, being as obstinate a man as his son described him. 'He, worn out by early hardship, was unfit for labour. My father's spirit was soon irritated, but not easily broken. There was a freedom in his lease in two years more, and to weather these we retrenched expences. We lived very poorly; I was a dexterous ploughman for my years; and the next eldest to me was a brother who could drive a plough very well and help me to thrash.' Robert reserved his most severe strictures for the factor, although it was his father who had condemned his sons to this appalling servitude for the full twelve years of the lease. 'My indignation yet boils at the recollection of the scoundrel tyrant's insolent, threatening epistles, which used to set us all in tears.'

Two years after his sojourn with Murdoch in Ayr, Robert enjoyed his next summer holiday. So it must have appeared to him by contrast with life at Mount Oliphant, although it was another intensive course of schooling. This time he was to learn mathematics at the school of Hugh Rodger of Kirkoswald, not far from Turnberry, where the crumbling castle in which King Robert Bruce was reared stood above the coast. The sixteen-year-old Robert was lodged on the farm of his uncle Samuel Broun, which evidently gave him greater latitude than when he had been constantly under the eye of John Murdoch in Ayr, and had even slept in the same bed with him.

So he recalled, describing the society of that coast of sailors and smugglers. 'The contraband trade was at that time very successful; scenes of swaggering riot and roaring dissipation were as yet new to me, and I was no enemy to social life.' Yet he persisted in his studies until another kind of distraction named Peggy Thomson crossed his path. 'I went on with a high hand in my geometry till the sun entered Virgo, a month which is always a carnival in my bosom. A charming Fillette who lived next door to the school overset my trigonometry and set me off in a tangent from the sphere of my studies.' He struggled on with his work for a few days more, but 'it was in vain to think of doing any more good at school. The remaining week I stayed I did nothing but craze the faculties of my soul about her, or steal out to meet with her'. Such was the second of the bard's innocent flirtations, and it was not surprising that he remembered it long, such a rare taste of happiness during those adolescent years in which his emotions were so cruelly starved. Peggy was married by the time he paid tribute to his 'once fondly loved and still remembered dear' in the first, Kilmarnock edition of his poems.

Like the pit ponies of old, that were taken back to the

mines after their brief summer scamper in the hills, Robert Burns returned to Mount Oliphant. There followed the final months of drudgery before the lease terminated and William Burness embarked on his final venture.

It began with greater promise than the previous one. He took a tenancy from a merchant of Ayr, not even committed to writing, of 130 acres about ten miles distant from Mount Oliphant, in the parish of Tarbolton. The property is called Lochlea, Lochlie in the old spelling, and as Robert was to remark, 'the nature of the bargain was such as to throw a little ready money in his hand at the commencement; otherwise the affair would have been impracticable'. It was a similar inducement that had encouraged him to take on Mount Oliphant, with an advance from Provost Fergusson. On this occasion disaster was postponed for four years, which have been described as perhaps the happiest that William's family ever enjoyed. The Alloway years may have been more carefree, but they left there before all seven children had been born. At any rate, Robert was to write, 'For four years we lived comfortably here.'

But during the early years at Lochlea Robert had the first recorded row with his father. If ever a son had earned the right to a little recreation, it was he, and at the age of twenty it was most natural that he should desire to learn to dance. Accordingly, 'to give my manners a brush, I went to a country dancing school. My father had an unaccountable antipathy against these meetings; and my going was, what to this hour I repent, in absolute defiance of his demands'. William Burness relented to the extent of allowing his other children to take dancing lessons as well, yet to his dying day he retained his antipathy to his eldest son. 'My father, as I said before, was a sport of strong passions; from that instance of rebellion he took a kind of dislike to me.'

It was in 1780, the year after this confrontation took place, that Robert wrote the earliest of his surviving letters. He had already been able to study this art for some time, ever since a brother of his mother's had brought back from Ayr an anthology of letters of Queen Anne's reign, including those of Pope and Bolingbroke. His first, addressed to his friend David Niven, was a rather self-conscious exercise, influenced by these models, and it was only gradually that one of the greatest letter-writers of this age mastered the medium. In doing so, he became his own best biographer, like that other superb letter-writer Lord Byron. Both were inspired by the discovery that they never met anyone as interesting as themselves, a

Lochlea. From a sepia drawing attributed to William Bartlett.
National Gallery of Scotland, Department of Prints and
Drawings.

Allan Ramsay (1686–1758). The Edinburgh wig-maker from Lanarkshire who turned bookseller, and opened the first circulating library in Scotland. His greatest service to literature was to edit the works of the Scots poets of an earlier age for publication, though his pastoral poems in the vernacular achieved another, in helping to inspire Fergusson and Burns.

judgment that posterity has endorsed in each case.

Of course he was also composing verses, and when he fell in love with a girl named Alison Begbie who worked on a neighbouring farm, he pressed his suit in prose as well as poetry. At least, it is assumed that his letters to 'My dear A.' were addressed to Alison; interesting evidence of her literacy. If, as has been surmised, his song for Mary Morison was inspired by Alison, then she was responsible for the best of its kind that he had yet composed.

> Yestreen when to the trembling string
> The dance gaed through the lighted ha',
> To thee my fancy took its wing:
> I sat, but neither heard nor saw.
> Though this was fair and that was [braw],   [fine]
> And yon the toast of a' the town,
> I sighed, and said amang them a',
> 'Ye are na Mary Morison.'
>
> *Mary Morison.*

According to the letters, Alison was the first girl to whom he made a formal proposal of marriage. When she declined, he wrote to her, 'It would be weak and unmanly to say that without you I never can be happy; but sure I am, that sharing life with you would have given it a relish that, wanting you, I can never taste.' In this strangely stilted manner ended the third of Robert's youthful infatuations. But they continued to feed the emotional fantasies which overflowed, throughout his life, in love songs that reveal only a tenuous connection with their object in so many cases.

It was at Lochlea that his poetry began to be influenced by the enthusiasm for the Scots tongue which had already seized a section of genteel society, aristocratic ladies in particular. To some extent this expressed itself in a sentimentally urban view of country life.

> The Lass of *Peattie*'s Mill,
> So bonny, blyth and gay,
> In spite of all my Skill,
> She stole my Heart away.
> When [tedding] of the Hay   [spreading]
> Bare-headed on the Green,
> Love 'midst her Locks did play,
> And wanton'd in her Een.

Allan Ramsay published those verses in Edinburgh decades before the birth of Burns, and they are not a fair sample of the work of the poet best known today as author of *The Gentle Shepherd*, though they probably reflect the taste of many of his readers. Ramsay was born at Leadhills in Lanarkshire, and came to Edinburgh as an adolescent, where he became a Burgess and founded what was probably the first circulating library in Britain, before 1728. Perhaps his greatest service to Scottish letters was to revive an interest in the poets of the past whose work constitutes the foundation for the Scots literary language.

He died in the year before the birth of Burns, to be followed by David Herd, with his *Ancient and Modern Scottish Songs*, published in 1769. But the most talented contributor to this literary movement was Robert Fergusson, who died three years before Burns came to Lochlea. He hailed from Tarland in Aberdeenshire, the son of a Baillie, his mother a Forbes, not of the line of baronets of Craigievar but of the branch of Tolquhon castle. After attending the university of St Andrews he became a clerk in an Edinburgh lawyer's office, and joined the convivial company of a club which included David Herd and the painters Runciman and Raeburn among its members. Here his dissipations contributed to the mental instability which led to his death in a lunatic asylum at the age of twenty-four, after sustaining a head injury in a fall.

Fergusson composed poetry in English with as much facility as James Thomson from Scotland and Oliver Goldsmith from Ireland, and might have been the equal of either in this medium if he had lived as long as they did. But he also embraced the fashion for the

*Robert Fergusson (1750–1774), who exercised a more profound
influence on Burns than any other poet. From the portrait by
Alexander Runciman. Scottish National Portrait Gallery,
Edinburgh.*

Alexander Pope. From the portrait, c. 1727, from the studio of M. Dahl. National Portrait Gallery, London.

Scottish vernacular, using both the literary sources and his knowledge of the Doric dialect of Aberdeenshire. Unfortunately he was ill fitted to meet the genteel taste for peasant themes, and his brilliant evocations of city life did not receive the critical acclaim they deserved. But it was precisely these poems that fired the imagination of Burns. When Fergusson did contribute to the country folk tradition, he did so with a taste that Burns was to find equally inspiring. Among his favourite songs is the one with the refrain:

> I'll meet thee on the lea-rig,
> My ain kind Dearie O.

Robert Fergusson had written:

> Will ye gang o'er the lea-rigg,
> My ain kind deary O!
> And cuddle there sae kindly
> Wi' me, my kind deary O?

> At thornie-dike and [birken-tree]   [birch]
> We'll [daff] and ne'er be weary O;   [flirt]
> They'll [scug ill een] frae you and me,
>   [turn askance]
> Mine ain kind deary O.

In the collection of poems published in the year before Fergusson's death, Burns could see the work of a man who could use standard English as competently as he could himself, yet chose also to write like that. And his admiration for the quality of this brilliant youth's style and thought must have exercised a powerful influence in his decision to do likewise.

Burns acknowledged his debt to Fergusson with all the generosity of his nature. Yet paradoxically, the kindred spirit he knew and admired was not closer to him, except in the language they used, than another bard whose poems he never heard. It has been observed that Fergusson's most precious legacy to him was the gift of satire. Four years before Fergusson's untimely death, during those early years at Lochlea, Rob Donn Mackay died in 1778 and was buried in Durness, in the far north-west of Scotland. Rob Donn too possessed an outstanding gift for satire, among all the others he shared with Robert Burns. But what they had most remarkably in common was a quality of punch. When Rob Donn praised the fine coat of a nobleman's son and concluded: 'but there isn't a button or a buttonhole in it that hasn't taken money off a poor man', it might be Burns speaking. He commented on a woman whose sexual habits were not the least of her shortcomings:

> I compared that wicked female
> With a ship that is damaged throughout,
> Whose prow they keep high and dry by pumping
> While the stern keeps letting it in.
>   *Translation by Ian Grimble.*

Burns could be as incisive and outspoken as that, but not more so. Even in *The Merry Muses of Caledonia*, his bawdy poems did not go farther than Rob Donn did when he described the reactions of women in the neighbourhood to a man who was running about in a state of indecent exposure, a 'streaker' as he would be called today. It is a laird's wife, specifically identified, who brings his adventure to an end when she calls out sportively, 'let a cloak be thrown over the devil's penis'.

The earliest English translations of Gaelic poetry to be published in Edinburgh had appeared in 1756, but there was none of Rob Donn's among them, and it is almost certain that Burns never heard of a bard to whom he bears a closer resemblance than even to Robert Fergusson, whose work he studied and admired. Indeed, the only literary link that can be discovered is the English satirist Alexander Pope, whose poetry and letters Burns certainly read in his youth, while in Durness Rob Donn's Minister, the Rev. Murdo MacDonald, was so liberal-minded as to translate passages of Pope into Gaelic for the benefit of his monoglot parishioners – of whom Rob Donn was one.

Here is an extraordinary paradox. There are 18th-century poets from the three different areas of Scotland, Sutherland in the far north, Ayrshire in the south-west, and Aberdeenshire in the north-east. They all display an outstanding gift for satire. This can be found elsewhere and earlier, both in the Gaelic and in the Scots literary traditions, but no cross-fertilization between them. The only literary connection between the two outstanding Scottish satirists of their age (and it is a most tenuous one) is Alexander Pope in Twicken-ham. As for the bogus Ossianic epics that Burns read, these are unrelieved by satire, although their author was a Gael, and knew the Ossianic folklore from which he extracted his plots as well as Rob Donn did. Pope proclaimed:

> Know then thyself, presume not God to scan,
> The proper study of mankind is man.

Robert Burns and Rob Donn followed this precept triumphantly, but whether or not Burns came across it in his reading, the Minister of Durness could hardly have poured such heresy into the ears of his flock. In the last resort it is a mystery, how a presiding spirit in 18th-century Scotland evoked reactions in two entirely different tongues from opposite ends of the country to almost every issue, religious, political and social, in many cases interchangeable.

Among those who knew Burns personally, more than one rated his conversation above his poetry. Maria Riddell wrote: 'Many others perhaps may have ascended to prouder heights in the region of Parnassus, but none certainly ever outshone Burns in the charms – the sorcery, I would almost call it, of fascinating conversation, the spontaneous eloquence of social argument, or the unstudied poignancy of brilliant repartee.' He found a new means of developing this art in November 1780, when the Tarbolton Bachelors' Club was formed.

Robert laid down the rules himself, and they may be read in a sense as the manifesto of the bard after he had come of age. The club was to meet once a month, to debate any subject except religion. No private conver-sation nor interruption was to be permitted during anyone's speech, and 'all swearing and profane language, and particularly all obscene and indecent conversation, is strictly prohibited'. The association was to be as much a training ground of manners as a forum for the practice of eloquence.

As to the qualifications for membership, 'Every man proper for a member of this Society must have a frank, honest, open heart; above anything dirty or mean; and must be a professed lover of one or more of the female sex. No haughty, self-conceited person, who looks upon himself as superior to the rest of the Club, and especially no mean-spirited, worldly mortal, whose only will is to heap up money, shall upon any pretence whatever be admitted. In short, the proper person for this Society is a cheerful, honest-hearted lad; who, if he has a friend that is true, and a mistress that is kind, and as much wealth as genteely to make both ends meet – is just as happy as this world can make him.' This is the earliest statement of Burns' polygamous attitude to women, which he was to demonstrate in practice on more than one occasion, although he was almost certainly still a virgin when he expressed it in these words.

At Tarbolton, the centre of the parish in which Lochlea lay, the club assembled for the first time in the home of John Richard, a two-storey house that has been preserved with care among all the other buildings associated with the poet. His brother Gilbert became a member with him, and Robert was elected President on the opening night, which fell on Hallowe'en. The question for debate was: 'Suppose a young man, bred a farmer, but without any fortune, has it in his power to marry either of two women, the one a girl of large fortune, but neither handsome in person nor agreeable in conversation, but who can manage the household affairs of a farm well enough; the other of them a girl every way agreeable, in person, conversation and behaviour, but without any fortune: which of them shall he choose?' The President of the Bachelors' Club, assessing his needs and his capacity, might well have been tempted to opt for both.

Among the members of the Bachelors' Club was young David Sillar, one of those local verse writers who add so greatly to the entertainment of their own communities during their lifetime, though they are generally of less interest to posterity. To Burns, so long starved of congenial male companionship, the dis-covery of a fellow-poet in the neighbourhood proved a most wonderful stimulus. Sillar later described their early acquaintance. 'We frequently met upon Sundays at church when, between sermons, instead of going with friends or lasses to the inn, we often took a walk in the fields.'

Perhaps David Sillar was recalling the Burns of a slightly later date in his next remark, not as to his appetite for the opposite sex, but the dexterity of his approach. 'In these walks I have frequently been struck by his facility in addressing the fair sex; and many times, when I have been bashfully anxious how to express myself, he would have entered into conver-sation with them with the greatest ease and freedom; and it was generally a death-blow to our conversation, however agreeable, to meet a female acquaintance.' Sillar observed that Burns did not seek to interest her in the subject of their talk. During these celibate years he was evidently more interested in their bodies than in their minds, as he was to remain for long after he had enjoyed possession of them.

However captivating the conversation of Robert Burns, it contained a flaw that was to damage his relationships throughout his life. Sillar was by no means the only acquaintance to mention it. 'His social disposition easily procured him acquaintance; but a certain satirical seasoning, with which he and all poetical geniuses are in some degree influenced, while it set the rustic circle in a roar, was not unaccompanied by its kindred attendant – suspicious fear.' When Rob Donn offered to reward the entertainment of Alexander Sage, the school-teacher of Tongue in Sutherland with a poem, the response was the same. The teacher's son Donald recalled, 'This offer my father declined, aware of those high powers of satire with which his guest was endowed, and which, like a razor dipped in oil, never cut so keenly as when intermingled with compliment and praise.' He might have been describing Burns. The Scotland of Holy Willies and pretentious men of letters engendered a spirit of satire from one end to the other, and of implacable resentment in its victims. If David Sillar was not the first to notice the effect of Robert's biting tongue, he was the earliest whose observation on the subject is recorded.

We are also indebted to Sillar for his description of the poet at Tarbolton. 'He wore the only tied hair in the parish, and in the church his plaid which was of a particular colour, I think *fillemot*, he wrapped in a particular manner around his shoulders.'

In July 1781 he was inducted into the St David's Lodge of Tarbolton as a Freemason. A writer who is not a member of this Order may perhaps be allowed to suggest that Freemasonry has been for centuries more integral to the fabric of Scottish society than to that of England. Whether or not English Freemasonry actually derives from Scotland, the earliest surviving documentation of the Order is to be found north of the Border. In taking this step, Robert Burns was placing himself within the protection of an organization that succours its members in time of need. But he was also enlarging his acquaintance in a most stimulating manner that was not in the least unconventional.

Such were the extending horizons of Burns's world when he enjoyed an even more formative experience in the summer of 1781.

Tarbolton, centre of the parish in which the farm of Lochlea lay.
Here Burns developed his outstanding gift for conversation in
the society of the Bachelors' Club. From Allan Cunnigham:
Pictures and Portraits of the Life and Land of Robert Burns, *1840.*

Chapter 2

IRVINE WAS ONE of the most ancient royal burghs in Scotland, its charter dating from early in the 13th century. When the 18th century opened it was still the country's third most important port, its harbour guarded by the Seagate castle. Today this stands some distance up the Irvine river, for shifting sands have altered the configuration of that coastline. But its many secret creeks still provided bases for profitable smuggling when Burns went to Irvine in 1781, particularly the illicit import of Irish grain.

As for the legitimate commerce of this port, it was being undermined gradually by the growth of other centres farther up the Clyde coast, especially Greenock. Captain Galt, owner of a West Indiaman, reflected this trend when he removed from Irvine to Greenock in 1789. By that time his son John was ten years old, and the formative years he had spent in Irvine during the period of Burns' sojourn there had influenced him for life. He made Irvine the setting for his novel *The Provost*, and the neighbouring village of Dreghorn the scene of his *Annals of the Parish*.

Both are ostensibly fiction, but they were accepted as authentic social history by no less an authority than G. M. Trevelyan, who described the *Annals* in particular as 'the most intimate and human picture of Scotland during her period of change in the reign of George III'. His judgment is confirmed by unpublished papers of the Earls of Elgin and Kincardine which Trevelyan did not see, and which provide the documentary evidence for a host of details that John Galt might otherwise have been thought to have invented. In these novels we experience life in an Ayrshire town and village exactly as Robert Burns did.

It has been observed that when Robert Burns did not compose in standard English he still employed English grammar, though he attached dialect terms to it in varying degrees. This is not surprising in one who was described as speaking extremely correct English, and who spent so much of his youth in the company of a father from Kincardineshire who perhaps never used

Irvine, still Scotland's third most important port when Burns went to stay there. From Wilson and Chambers: The Land of Burns. *Engraving by D. O. Hill.*

John Galt (1779–1839), whose upbringing in Irvine inspired his novels The Provost *and* Annals of the Parish, *which G. M. Trevelyan described as 'the most intimate and human picture of Scotland' during the lifetime of Burns. From an engraving by T. Woolnoth from the painting by E. Hastings.*

an Ayrshire expression in his life, even though he heard his wife Agnes Broun using them in the house.

It was during his comparatively brief visits to Ayr, Kirkoswald and Tarbolton that Burns would have heard the speech of this region. Evidently, like the poetry of Robert Fergusson, it was music to his ears though he had not been brought up on it and never attempted to use it consistently except in a single letter.

Robert had been sent by his father to Irvine to master one of the processes in the conversion of flax into linen. This was one of the growth industries of the 18th century. Among its pioneers was the great Daniel Campbell of Shawfield, who purchased Islay and introduced flax among his other measures to improve the island's economy. After his death in 1753 a grandson wrote: 'To the branch of the flax industry and manufacture he turned his care and attention. He laid out in building lint milns, bringing to the island manufacturers, hecklers, weavers etc, considerably above £2,000 sterling.' That was a great deal more money than it is today. The produce of Islay would arrive by sea at the Clyde ports for bleaching.

Beyond the Firth of Clyde, within sight of Islay, the prosperity of Ulster was built upon the expanding linen industry. It continued to flourish into the present century and today its buildings are carefully preserved, the thatched mills that used wind and water power, the larger brick mills that employed steam power, some of them now converted to other purposes. William Burness was moving with the times when he leased about three acres of his land to his sons Robert and Gilbert to grow flax. When the results proved promising, he determined to carry the experiment further, for higher profits went to those who continued the manufacturing process themselves rather than disposing of the raw product. There was the softening of the flax by soaking it in water, the retting process. There was the stripping of the outer husk, leaving the linen fibres exposed, the hackling stage; spinning into yarn, weaving into linen, bleaching.

In a hackling shop, perhaps in the High Street of Irvine, in association with a man named Peacock, possibly a relative of his mother's, Robert Burns learnt the tedious and arduous task that was intended to bring good fortune to his father at last. This new form of indoor labour contributed to the first attack of his heart disease that Robert described in his own words. Writing to his father on 27 December, he confessed, 'The weakness of my nerves has so debilitated my mind that I dare not either review past events, or look forward into futurity; for the least anxiety, or perturbation in my breast, produces most unhappy effects on my whole frame. Sometimes, indeed, when, for an hour or two, as is sometimes the case, my spirits are a little lightened, I glimmer a little into futurity; but my principal, and indeed my only pleasurable enjoyment is looking backwards and forwards in a moral and religious way. I am quite transported at the thought that ere long, perhaps very soon, I shall bid an eternal adieu to all the pains, and uneasiness and disquietude of this weary life.' At least his devout father could derive satisfaction from the state of his soul.

Robert took to composing religious verses that tell of the pain and despondency he suffered.

Sure Thou, Almighty, canst not act
From cruelty or wrath!
O free my weary eyes from tears
Or close them fast in death!

But if I must afflicted be
To suit some wise design,
Then, man my soul with firm resolves
To bear and not repine!
A Prayer, Under the Pressure of Violent Anguish.

He was using a verse form of the metrical psalms which Speaker Rous the Cornishman had produced during the great rebellion of the previous century, introduced into Scotland after the Presbyterian party had adopted the Westminster Confession of Faith. He would use the same metres a great deal more effectively for a satirical purpose later.

In describing the misery of those months in Irvine, Burns called his complaint hypochondria, not realising that this was only an effect on his spirits of a physical condition. 'The finishing evil that brought up the rear of this infernal file,' he was to recall, 'was my hypochondriac complaint being irritated to such a degree, that for three months I was in a diseased state of mind and body.' But by then he was referring also to the disaster that had occurred a few days after his despondent letter to his father. 'My partner was a scoundrel of the first water who made money by the mystery of thieving; and to finish the whole, while we were giving a welcome carousal to the New Year, our shop, by the drunken carelessness of my partner's wife, took fire and was burnt to ashes.'

But before Robert returned to Lochlea in the spring of 1782, in the aftermath of the latest fiasco, he gained a new friend in Irvine. His name was Richard Brown, and Burns was to describe him in such terms as he never bestowed on another. Brown was at least as well educated as he, and he had seen the world as Robert had not. Taking to the sea, he had been put ashore on the coast of Connaught in Ireland where he was robbed of everything he possessed, so that he had also known misfortune.

'This gentleman's mind was fraught with courage, independence and magnanimity, and every noble virtue,' Burns wrote of him. 'I loved him, I admired him, to a degree of enthusiasm; and I strove to imitate him. In some measure I succeeded. I had the pride before, but he taught it to flow in proper channels. His knowledge of the world was vastly superior to mine, and I was all attention to learn. He was the only man I ever saw who was a greater fool than myself when WOMAN was the presiding star; but he spoke of a certain fashionable failing with levity, which hitherto I

The breaking and scutching process. The growing of flax for manufacture into linen was a major 18th-century industry. Burns went to Irvine in 1781 to study its methods. A drawing of 1783.

The house at which Burns stayed in Irvine. Anonymous drawing, 1784.

'The simple Bard, rough at the rustic plough,
Learning his tuneful trade from ev'ry bough.'
The far from simple Burns, taken literally in the Burns
Centenary issue of The Illustrated London News, *1859.*

had regarded with horror. Here his friendship did me a mischief.'

Did it really? Burns the superb autobiographer could arrange his material for dramatic effect. For instance, he attributed his despondency in Irvine partly to the fact that he had been jilted by Alison Begbie. This would have been wholly uncharacteristic. It has been observed that with Burns, absence never made the heart grow fonder, and that he was soon consoled for the disappearance of one girl by the appearance of another. As to whether it needed a Richard Brown to lead him astray into the paths of fornication, this is at least questionable. In later years Captain Brown, a respectable family man, objected strongly to the imputation. A more likely culprit, one might suppose, was William Burness, whose repressive influence had stifled the perfectly natural appetites of his son beyond his twenty-third year, the best possible recipe for the sexual explosion that was to come. Perhaps it also contributed to Robert's lifelong inability to experience the emotion of being in love with a woman, although he spent so much of his time describing it in general terms in verse. 'I conceive love to be that which will never alter,' observed Rob Donn.

Burns could not have said that; or if he could have said it, he could not have meant it so far as his own feelings were concerned.

But evidently Richard Brown provided just the tonic that Burns needed to raise his spirits. Years later, when the publication of his poems had made him famous, he gave Brown the credit for encouraging him in this other activity which he coupled with Love as his highest enjoyment. 'You told me, on my repeating some verses to you, that you wondered I could resist the temptation of sending verses of such merit to a magazine: 'twas actually this that gave me the idea of my own pieces which encouraged me to endeavour at the character of a Poet.'

What is most extraordinary is that neither the friendship of this sailor nor the activities of the busy port of Irvine gave Burns the slightest interest in the life of the sea or the spectacle of the ocean in its many moods. Rob Donn too was a landsman, but he composed a dramatic account of a crossing of the Minch in a storm. He did not fail to describe the kelp-boat in which a goat-herd carried his cheeses along the coast, the old skiff that was wrecked on the rocks, the flat-bottomed fishing craft with square stern called a coble.

Isn't the new coble beautiful
With Ranald's daughter at the helm?
Translation by Ian Grimble.

Robert Burns, during the Lochlea period, did introduce the sea as a background to a poem in which he swore eternal fidelity to some passing flame. But the allusion has the vagueness of a passage in MacPherson's Ossian.

From thee, Eliza, I must go,
And from my native shore:
The cruel fates between us throw
A boundless ocean's roar;
But boundless oceans, roaring wide,
Between my Love and me,
They never, never can divide
My heart and soul from thee.

Song, to the tune, *Gilderoy.*

Nature ashore likewise served for the most part as a mere background to the bard's exploration of the lives of people and animals, and of his own emotions, although here it was treated in far more specific detail. His friend David Sillar did describe him at this time as delighting in his natural surroundings. 'Some of the few opportunities of a noontide walk that a country life allows her laborious sons he spent on the banks of the river, or in the neighbourhood of the woods of Stair.' But he was not 'learning his tuneful trade from every bough', like the unlettered peasant he pretended to be. He was reading a book which, as Sillar tells us, 'he always carried, and read when not otherwise employed'.

Wordsworth enjoyed a comparatively brief glimpse of the Arran peaks, rising beyond the waters of the Firth of Clyde, and described what he saw. Burns never mentioned them. Perhaps James Thomson would not have celebrated nature for its own sake in *The Seasons* if he had remained in his rural surroundings rather than settling in London. Scotland's greatest 18th-century nature poet, Duncan Macintyre, might not have celebrated his native Glenorchy with such affection if he had not spent half his life in the city of Edinburgh.

My blessings on the deer forests –
O they are marvellous mountains,
With green cress and spring water,
A noble, royal, delightful drink –
On the beloved moorlands
And the plentiful pastures.

Translation by Ian Grimble.

Burns was to speak with a different voice from any of these, Thomson, Rob Donn or Macintyre, and he found this voice during the years at Lochlea, and very wonderful it is. There is no need to complain about what it is not.

Characteristic of the introspective vein in which he excelled is the song, *My father was a farmer upon the Carrick border O*, set to the tune of 'The weaver and his

shuttle O'. It is an early equivalent of his autobiographical letters, alternating between despondency, fortitude and hope as he relates the ups and downs of his life, unaware that these moods were caused as much by his heart disease as by the buffetings of fortune. His father had bred him up 'in decency and order', and taught him that 'without an honest manly heart, no man was worth regarding'. It says much for the magnanimity of his injured heart that he could seek out and celebrate these grounds for gratitude to his father.

'My talents they were not the worst; nor yet my education O'. Yet all his labours had ended in failure, and he could see no better prospects in the future.

Thus all obscure, unknown, and poor, thro' life
I'm doom'd to wander, O
Till down my weary bones I lay in everlasting
slumber O.

Yet he can still enjoy today, whatever the morrow may bring, still enjoy people for their real worth, rather than their wealth or social position.

Had you the wealth Potosi boasts, or nations to
adore you, O
A cheerful honest-hearted clown I will prefer
before you. O

Back in Lochlea he continued his reading, as he described in a letter to his former teacher John Murdoch, telling him how he was revelling in 'sentimental' authors, in the elegies of Shenstone, in the poetry of James Thomson, in the novel of Henry Mackenzie, *The Man of Feeling*, 'a book I prize next to the Bible, Man of the World, Sterne, especially his Sentimental Journey, MacPherson's Ossian, etc.' How well he escaped the influence of MacPherson's flatulence and Mackenzie's tear-jerking sensibility, Burns demonstrated in his poem on the death of poor Mailie.

She was a pet ewe, that Robert bought with her two lambs and tethered in a field beside his home. His brother Gilbert described the episode which prompted Robert's verses. 'He and I were going out with our teams, and our two younger brothers to drive for us, at midday, when Hugh Wilson, a curious-looking, awkward boy clad in a plaiding, came to us with much anxiety in his face, with the information that the ewe had entangled herself in the tether, and was lying in the ditch. Robert was much tickled with Huoc's appearance and posture on the occasion. Poor Mailie was set to rights, and when we returned from the plough in the evening he repeated to me her *Death and Dying Words* pretty much in the way they now stand.'

It is an extraordinary characteristic of sheep that they will lie on their backs in a ditch until they die, whether tangled in a tether or not, without attempting to extricate themselves even when birds light on them and pluck out their eyes. Yet a human can galvanize them into doing so, if he finds them in time, without so

'Twill make a man forget his woe,
And heighten all his joy;
'Twill make the widow's heart to sing
Tho' the tear were in her eye.

Finis—I don't like the Above but
Perhaps I am wrong

yowe }
pet ewe
The death & dyin' words o' poor Mailie— my ain
an unco mournfu' Tale.

printed—
Creech—
As Mailie & her lambs thegither
Were ae day nibblin' on the tether,
Upon her cloot she coost a hitch
And o'er she warsl'd in the ditch.
There dying groanin', dyin' she did lye
When Hughoc he cam' doitin' bye.

Wi' glowrin' een & lifted hands
Poor Hughoc like a statue stands;
He saw her days were near hand ended,
But waes=my=heart, he could na mend it;
He gaped wide, but naething spak,
At length poor Mailie silence brak—

O Thou whase lamentable face
Appears to mourn my woefu' case,
My dyin' words attentive hear
And bear them to my Master dear.
Tell him if e'er again he keep
As muckle gear as buy a sheep,
O bid him never tye them mair
Wi' wicked strings o' hemp or hair;
But ca' them out to park or hill
And let them wander at their will.
So may his flock increase & grow
To scores o' lambs & packs o' woo'

Page 24 of Burns's first Commonplace Book, 1783–1785, in which the bard spelt his name 'Burness'. The poem describing the death of Poor Mailie, his pet ewe.

much as touching them. Mailie was 'set to rights', but Burns imagines that she perished after uttering her last words to Hughoc.

> Wi' [glow'rin] een, an' lifted han's,   [gazing intently]
> Poor *Hughoc* like a statue stan's;
> He saw her days were near hand ended,
> But, waes my heart! he could na mend it!
> He gaped wide, but naething spak,
> At length poor *Mailie* silence brak.

The message that Mailie sends to her master through Hughoc is a masterpiece of mock-sentimentality, both moving and funny.

> Tell him, he was a Master kin',
> An' ay was guid to me an' mine;
> An' now my *dying* charge I gie him,
> My helpless *lambs*, I trust them wi' him.

She gives instructions for their upbringing, not forgetting the morals of her 'son and heir,' who is to be warned 'to stay content wi' *yowes* [ewes] at hame.' Finally she sends a farewell message to both son and daughter.

> And now, *my bairns*, wi' my last breath,
> I lea'e my blessin wi' you baith:
> An' when ye think upo' your Mither,
> Mind to be kind to ane anither.
> Now, honest *Hughoc*, dinna fail,
> To tell my Master a' my tale;
> An' bid him burn this cursed *tether*,
> An' for thy pains thou'se get my
>   [blather].'   [bladder]

> This said, poor Mailie turned her head,
> An' closed her een amang the dead!
> *The Death and Dying Words of Poor Mailie.*

Another poem about Mailie informs us that 'her forbears were brought in ships frae 'yont the Tweed', so that she was of the Cheviot breed.

The Burness family needed all the entertainment Robert could give them to lighten their spirits, for in the autumn after his return home in 1782 his father was overcome by his final disaster. He had made no written tenancy agreement with David McLure, the merchant of Ayr who was proprietor of Lochlea, and now there was a dispute over the share that each should pay towards the cost of improvements. The matter was submitted to arbitration, the representatives of the two men could not agree, and so a third man was brought in as referee.

His ruling was that of the £775 which McLure claimed from William Burness, £543 was deductable for rent payments and improvement costs, and this ought to have been the end of the matter. But the arbitration had dragged on until August 1783 before this verdict was reached, and McLure had anticipated

Country life in Scotland in the 18th century. The young man has been frightened by tales of a witch. An illustration from Allan Ramsay's The Gentle Shepherd, *illustrated by David Allan for an edition of 1796.*

it by obtaining a writ of sequestration on the produce of Lochlea farm, hoping thereby to gain the whole amount to which he believed he was entitled. William Burness responded by taking the case to the Court of Session. His family must have been aghast as they witnessed his failing health, undermined by tuberculosis and anxiety, and faced with the prospect of destitution. But the greatest burden of worry fell on Robert, who would be left to shoulder the burden of supporting a widowed mother and six younger brothers and sisters.

From these miseries he escaped when he could into his private world. Betty Davidson had told him about it as a child: Richard Brown had directed him to it. In April 1783 he began his first Commonplace Book, still calling himself Robert Burness like his family before him, although his name had been entered in the baptismal register as Burns. He described it as an anthology of 'Observations, Hints, Songs, Scraps of Poetry etc.' and delineated the author as 'a man who had little art in making money, and still less in keeping it; but was, however, a man of some sense, a great deal of honesty, and unbounded good-will to every creature rational or irrational'. Here the pose of the unlettered peasant makes an early appearance. 'As he was but little indebted to scholastic education, and bred at a plough-tail, his performances must be strongly tinctured with his unpolished, rustic way of life; but as I believe, they are really his own, it may be some entertainment to a curious observer of human nature to see how a ploughman thinks and feels, under the pressure of Love, Ambition, Anxiety, Grief with the like cares and passions; which, however diversified by the Modes and Manners of life, operate pretty much alike, I believe, in all the Species.'

In his Commonplace Book he entered his own poetry, with illuminating comments. He was apologetic about his earliest recorded song, in praise of Nelly Kirkpatrick, though few juvenilia have been better. He introduced his religious verses with the explanation: 'There was a certain period of my life that my spirit was broke by repeated losses and disasters which threatened, and indeed effected, the utter ruin of my fortune. My body was attacked by that most dreadful distemper, a hypochondria, or confirmed melancholy. In this wretched state, the recollection of which makes me yet shudder, I hung my harp on the willow trees, except in some lucid intervals, in one of which I composed the following.' We should remember this passage, when faced with the relatively small output of original poetry during his last years.

Robert described his poem 'My father was a farmer upon the Carrick Border O' as 'a wild rhapsody miser-ably deficient in versification'. It might be thought that much of his rhyming only appears defective because it is not spelt in a way that renders the pronunciation of the dialect in which it is composed. In certain cases this is so. But all his life Burns subordinated the demands of correct rhyming to what he wanted to say. The idea and its proper expression were what mattered to him; the target, and the arrow that whizzed straight to its bull's-eye. A suitable decoration of his thoughts, whether in tartan or frock-coat, fortunately concerned him less. The particular kind of magic he achieved in his poetry owes much to his instinctive sense of the relative importance of form and content.

At this time Robert wrote to John Murdoch, 'I seem to be one sent into the world to see and observe; I easily compound with the knave who tricks me of my money, if there be anything original about him which shows me human nature in a different light from anything I have seen before. In short, the joy of my heart is to "study men, their manners and their ways".' In the

---

The grave of the poet's father in the cemetery of the Auld Kirk of Alloway. The first headstone, placed there by Robert Burns, was chipped away by souvenir hunters, and this is the third. Scottish Tourist Board.

Commonplace Book there is the first intimation of his unfulfilled ambition to write a play, a fragment of blank verse 'intended for a tragedy'. But although his observation of others was as keen as Byron's, it appears likely that any play he might have written would have been, like those of Byron, largely centred on himself.

The subject of his dramatic lines was remorse, and he commented on them: 'I entirely agree with that judicious philosopher Mr Smith in his excellent Theory of Moral Sentiments, that remorse is the most painful sentiment that can embitter the human bosom', and more to the same effect. In fact his Commonplace Book reflects more on his reading than on his personal observations of human nature, as in this reference to Adam Smith. He continued adding to it from 1783 until 1785, a traumatic period of his life.

The family were comforted by the medical attentions of Dr John Mackenzie, a Freemason, though he could offer them no hope of William's recovery. Mackenzie was one of those who recognized a talent in Robert that others were to rate even higher than his poetry. 'Before I was acquainted with his poetical powers, I perceived that he possessed very great mental abilities, an uncommonly fertile and lively imagination.' He could only have discovered this through the bard's conversation, and he said as much, like so many others who were spellbound by it. 'I have always thought that no person could have a just idea of the extent of Burns' talents who had not an opportunity to hear him converse.' Yet this man, who admired him so much, was to rank next to the bard's father as the cause of his death, so little was the disease of endocarditis understood in his time, even in the country that by now led Europe in medical science.

Advised by Dr Mackenzie that the end was near, Robert wrote to his first cousin in Montrose, James Burness, to inform him that his father was 'in a dying condition'. He sent William's greetings, 'probably for the last time in this world'. The correspondence is noteworthy in two respects. A man who liked to pose as an unlettered peasant when he was already one of the most cultivated letter-writers in Scotland was addressing a relative who was a lawyer. And he expressed himself on the subject of his father's condition with chilling brevity. Clearly the approach of death had not engendered any spirit of reconciliation between William and his eldest son.

All the same, the final act of cruelty of the dying man still appals. The family took turns in watching at his bedside, and Robert and his sister Isabella were with him on the morning of 13 February 1784 when William roused himself to deliver his final homily to her. He urged her to walk in the paths of righteousness, then rambled on with the reflection that there was one of his children about whom he had misgivings. Robert stepped to his bedside and asked, 'Is it me you mean?' The old man told him it was. Robert turned to the window to hide his tears, an episode that remained vivid in his

sister's memory. A few hours later their father had joined the uninviting, by no means overcrowded, company of the Elect in the Calvinist paradise.

Almost within the year Burns had composed *Holy Willie's Prayer*. It was attributed to a specific person, a sanctimonious Elder of the neighbouring parish of Mauchline. But his intimate understanding of such a person's religious attitude may well have been fashioned nearer home.

> O thou that in the heavens does dwell!
> Wha, as it pleases best thysel,
> Sends ane to heaven and ten to h–ll,
>   A' for thy glory!
> And no for ony gude or ill
>   They've done before thee. –
>
> I bless and praise thy matchless might,
> When thousands thou has left in night,
> That I am here before thy sight,
>   For gifts and grace,
> A burning and a shining light
>   To a' this place. –

Dr Mackenzie found William Burness frigid, reserved and vacuous: his wife doted on him in admiration. He had overworked his family, and would have left them destitute but for the steps taken by a son whom he had maltreated in almost every way open to him. He had indeed done his best to educate Robert, as it was customary to do in Scotland in his time, the country then enjoying the highest standard of general education in Europe. For the rest, it was he who gave life to Robert Burns, and who took it from him.

During the period of acute anxiety when William was dying, and the case before the Court of Session remained to be decided, another Freemason lent his assistance to the distressed family. He was a lawyer of Mauchline named Gavin Hamilton whose broad-minded religious views exposed him to the censure of Holy Willie, the Elder. He acted as factor (or estate manager) to the Earl of Loudoun, from whom he had leased the 118–acre farm of Mossgiel, two miles from Lochlea. This he offered to lease to Robert and his brother Gilbert for £90 a year, a far more favourable rent than any their father had obtained, so providing them with an asylum in case they were rendered homeless.

Gavin Hamilton also suggested a stratagem designed to give William's family priority as creditors on the assets of Lochlea farm. His sons had been given the status of wage-earning labourers there, and Hamilton recommended that the daughters should be enrolled retrospectively in the same manner. This was sharp practice, but McClure had shown equally little scruple in taking out his writ of sequestration, which led to the ruinous court proceedings. William learnt that he had won his case a few weeks before he died, but it was a hollow victory since it had swallowed the last of his savings. With Hamilton's help and Robert's canny connivance the family were able to move to

Mossgiel, relatively well provided for, a month after the bard had succeeded as its head.

By this time he had celebrated his emancipation by throwing his celibacy to the winds. His accomplice was a young girl from Largieside who acted as home help to Agnes Broun during her husband's last illness. She was considered coarse and unattractive, except for her figure. But she was available, which was of considerably more importance to Robert than her appearance as he flung himself upon her. He could always improve her charms in verse.

> My girl she 's airy, she's buxom and gay,
> Her breath is as sweet as the blossoms in May;
>   A touch of her lips it ravishes quite.
> She 's always good natur'd, good humor'd and
>   free;
> She dances, she glances, she smiles with a glee;
>   Her eyes are the lightenings of joy and
>   delight:
> Her slender neck, her handsome waist,
> Her hair well buckl'd, her stays well lac'd,
> Her taper white leg with an et, and a, c,
> For her a, b, e, d, and her c, u, n, t,
>   And Oh, for the joys of a long winter night!!!
>   *Song*, to the tune, *Black Joke*.

It has been suggested that William Burness may have observed Robert's flirtation with Elizabeth Paton, and that this was what provoked his last words to his son.

This cannot be disproved, but it appears improbable. The sick room of the dying man was not the most promising setting for a seduction, and anyway Burns may be credited with more sense. It is at least as plausible to suppose that his father had noticed over a far longer period what everyone else did; that Robert was a bewitching talker, who expressed himself with a free-thinking candour that could scandalize the orthodox, and with a satirical gift that aroused personal resentment. If, as is likely, he had begun to usurp the authority of his rather pontifical father at his own board, William's jealousy and resentment are easily accountable. But again, this is speculation.

Gilbert Burns described the new order at Mossgiel. 'Every member of the family was allowed ordinary wages for the labour performed on the farm. My brother's allowance and mine was seven pounds per annum each. And during the whole time this family concern lasted, which was four years, as well as during the period at Lochlea, his expences never in any one year exceeded his slender income. As I was entrusted with the keeping of the family accounts, it is not possible that there can be any fallacy in this statement, in my brother's favour. His temperence and frugality were everything that could be wished.' Robert had

---

Mossgiel. The farmhouse kitchen, from a wash drawing by William Allan. National Gallery of Scotland, Department of Prints and Drawings.

given the lie to his father's misgivings, in stepping forward as a devoted and conscientious head of the family in his place. So he was to prove for the remainder of his life.

In defending his brother against the charge of drunkenness, Gilbert was contradicting Robert himself. When the bard drew up his rules for the Tarbolton Bachelors, he stipulated, 'no member is to spend more than threepence on drink'. His own pocket could not have borne more, as Gilbert confirmed, but neither could his physical condition. Loving male company as he did, he once confessed, 'they will not have me if I do not drink with them, and every time I give them a slice of my constitution'. This is the opposite to the language of an alcoholic.

Yet he liked to pose as a merry drinker, and more than once wrote a letter in which he boasted that he was intoxicated, although the terms in which he expressed himself prove that he was sober. He dated his dissipations back to the weeks in Kirkoswald, when he was a teenager living with his uncle, the tenant farmer Samuel Broun. 'The contraband trade was at that time very successful; scenes of swaggering riot and roaring dissipation were as yet new to me, and I was no enemy to social life. Here, though, I learned to look unconcerned on a large tavern bill, and mix without fear in a drunken squabble.' He paid the price after his death when his letters fell into the hands of a biographer who was a teetotaller and temperance fanatic, and took him at his word.

But James Hogg the Border poet, who was his younger contemporary, knew better and confirmed the testimony of Gilbert. 'Burns has been accused of inveterate dissipation and drunkenness. Nonsense! Burns was no more a drunkard than I am; nay, I would bet that on an average I drink double what he did; and yet I am acknowledged both in Scotland and in England as a most temperate and cautious man; and so I am.' Possessed of a soaring imagination, Burns broke the shackles of his arduous and humdrum life in flights of fancy, and this was one of them.

The reality at Mossgiel was less poetic. 'I entered on this farm,' Robert recalled, 'with a full resolution, "Come, go to, I will be wise!" I read farming books; I calculated crops; I attended markets; and in short, in spite of "the devil, the world and the flesh," I believe I would have been a wise man. But the first year, from unfortunately buying in bad seed, the second from a late harvest, we lost half of both our crops. This overset all my wisdom, and I returned "Like a dog to his vomit, and the sow that was washed to her wallowing in the mire."'

It is hard to decide what was chiefly responsible for this latest misfortune, apart from the weather. Even if Mossgiel needed draining, Gavin Hamilton had given a tenancy on generous terms, and it is likely that he was equally indulgent over the price of the stock, about which Burns had written to him before the family moved. 'As you were pleased to give us the offer of a

James Hogg, 'The Ettrick Shepherd' (1770–1835). Of Burns's reputation for drunkenness he observed, 'Nonsense! Burns was no more a drunkard than I am.'

private bargain of your cows you intend for sale, my brother and I this day took a look of them with a friend with us on whose judgment we could something depend, to enable us to form an estimate. If you are still intending to let us have them in that way, please appoint a day that we may wait on you and either agree amongst ourselves or else fix men to whom we may refer it.' One wonders whether Robert depended on his own judgment when he bought inferior seed, or that of the friend he mentioned in this letter.

When Robert wrote of the dog returning to its vomit and the sow to the mire, it is difficult to avoid the conclusion that he was referring to anyone other than Elizabeth Paton of the slender neck and handsome waist. Extraordinary though this may appear, he was later to speak of the girl he married in scabrous and affectionate terms almost in the same breath. Suffice to say, Paton had gone back to her home in Largieside when the family moved to Mossgiel in March 1784. Since her daughter was not born until 22 May 1785, it follows that the father must have resumed relations with her at least by the previous September. The sow's partner certainly received a washing in the interval, the most serious attack of his illness that Burns had suffered yet, for which Dr Mackenzie prescribed a cold bath beside his bed, into which the patient was ordered to plunge when one of his fainting fits began. He was also advised to take strenuous exercise when complete rest would have been the correct treatment.

There is a gap in the Commonplace Book between April and August 1784, which suggests that the latest relapse lasted even longer than Robert's illness in Irvine. Yet he was evidently fit enough to be installed as Depute-Master of the St James Lodge of Free-

'The sweetest hours that e'er I spend,
Are spent amang the lasses, O.'
From Allan Cunningham: Pictures and Portraits of the Life and
Land of Robert Burns, *1840.*

masons in the July of that year, an office he held until the end of 1786. During the summer he was also frequenting Mauchline, making new friends there and eyeing the girls. By now a tenant farmer in his own right, he was known by his property as Robert Mossgiel according to the custom of the country, and beginning to dramatize himself as a rake as well as a drunkard.

> O leave novels, ye Mauchline belles,
> Ye're safer at your spinning wheel;
> Such witching books are baited hooks
> For rakish rooks like Rob Mossgiel.

Perhaps it was by comparison with these that poor Elizabeth Paton's charms lost their lustre, giving Robert the feeling that he was returning like a dog to its vomit.

> Beware a tongue that's smoothly hung;
> A heart that warmly seems to feel;
> That feelin heart but acks a part,
> 'Tis rakish art in Rob Mossgiel.
> The frank address, the soft caress,
> Are worse than poisoned darts of steel,
> The frank address, and politesse,
> Are all finesse in Rob Mossgiel.
>
> *O leave novels, ye Mauchline belles.*

He could be disingenuous on the one hand, and on the other startlingly candid. Although he was no more a rake than he was a drunkard, he could certainly play the part of a cad with women, and he boasted of the fact with unabashed honesty. It has been observed that the kind of women who attracted him sexually often find this irresistible in the male.

Burns was a young man of twenty-five who would almost certainly have boasted of the fact if he had ever been to bed with more than a single girl. The rest was bravado and wishful thinking, which received considerable encouragement when he met Jean Armour during that summer of 1784. She was nineteen years old, the daughter of the respectable master mason James Armour, whose house of red sandstone still stands among so many that the bard frequented in Mauchline. A solemn, devout man, he had heeded the Old Testament injunction to be fruitful and multiply, to the tune of eleven children.

Legend relates that Burns was at a dance when his collie came to him, standing by himself. He remarked that he wished he could find a girl who would show him so much affection, and was overheard by Jean. A few days later she called to him across the green, asking him laughingly whether he had found the girl he was looking for yet. Jean herself testified that she made the first advance, so the apocryphal story may be true. By the following summer he was recalling in his Common-place Book:

When first I came to Stewart Kyle
My mind it was nae steady,
Where e'er I gaed, where e'er I rade,
A Mistress still I had ay:
But when I came roun' by Mauchlin town,
Not dreadin' anybody,
My heart was caught before I thought
And by a Mauchlin Lady.

A Fragment, to the tune,
I had a horse and I had nae mair –

He was a father by the time he wrote that, whenever he composed it. Characteristically, he was proud of his sexual prowess, gave little further thought to the mother, and expressed all his affection for his child. In this at least, his emotions were those of a family man.

Welcome! My bonie, sweet, wee Dochter!
Tho' ye come here a wee unsought for;
And tho' your comin I hae fought for,
    Baith Kirk and Queir;
Yet by my faith, ye're no unwrought for,
    That I shall swear!

For if thou be, what I wad hae thee,
And tak the counsel I shall gie thee,
I'll never rue my trouble wi' thee,
    The cost nor shame o't,
But be a loving Father to thee,
    And brag the name o't. –

*A Poet's Welcome
to his love-begotten Daughter.*

His mother took custody of the child, and he was as good as his word.

Another poem that he wrote in his Commonplace Book before the collapse of his health in April 1784 was portentous.

There's nought but care on eve'ry han',
    In ev'ry hour that passes, O:
What signifies the life o' man,
    An' 'twere na for the lasses, O.

*Green grow the rashes, O;
Green grow the rashes, O;
The sweetest hours that e'er I spend,
Are spent amang the lasses, O.
    Green grow the Rashes. A Fragment.*

This is an early example of Burns' skill in emending or rewriting an old folk-song; sometimes, as in this case, making a bawdy one respectable. A year or so later he sent three verses of the indecent version to his friend John Richmond.

Green grow the rashes, O,
Green grow the rashes, O,
The lasses they hae wimble bores,
The widows they hae gashes O.

Richmond was a nineteen-year-old lawyer's clerk in the office of Gavin Hamilton when Burns made his acquaintance, and he was to become the most intimate of all the bard's friends in Mauchline. To some extent this was the relationship between Burns and Richard Brown in Irvine with the roles reversed, young John Richmond the admiring disciple of the older, more experienced farmer of Mossgiel. They were joined by another acolyte who was also six years younger than Burns, a linen draper of the village named James Smith. Whether or not Richard Brown had led Burns astray in the paths of fornication as he accused the sailor of doing, Burns certainly seems to have encouraged these two youths of Mauchline, until both were compelled to leave the parish. One of the most accomplished of the bard's bawdy poems relates the proceedings of a Court of Equity, at which Burns sits as judge with Smith as the Fiscal and Richmond 'our trusty Clerk, our minutes regular to mark, and sit dispenser of the law.' They try two men who have stained 'the fornicator's honour', one by denying his deed, the other by attempting to procure an abortion.

In selecting the company of relatively immature youths whose intellectual gifts were deeply inferior to his own, Burns was not making the best of the limited social opportunities open to him. He also enjoyed the friendship of Robert Aiken of Ayr, who was twenty years older than the bard; as well as those Mauchline Freemasons Gavin Hamilton and Dr Mackenzie. He cultivated more earthy society because it was congenial to him. He was to do the same later, when he went to Edinburgh at the height of his fame, with serious consequences for his career.

Since the years he spent at Mossgiel in the parish of Mauchline were the most productive in his life as a poet, this remains the heartland of the society that Burns immortalized. Although the village church that witnessed such dramas was replaced in the 19th century, many of the surrounding buildings of his time are still there to see; the home of Dr Auld the Minister, of Gavin Hamilton, Dr Mackenzie and James Armour. Here is Poosie Nansie's inn, the hostelry kept by Agnes Gibson, whose far from blameless daughter was known as Racer Jess in testimony of the speed with which she ran errands for a consideration. It was here that the gathering of *The Jolly Beggars* occurred.

Long after the poet's death John Richmond gave an account to Robert Chambers of the event which inspired the poem. Since he was in the company of Burns and James Smith when they visited Poosie Nansie's and found the beggars there, it probably dates from the days of the Court of Equity. But Burns did not write it into his first Commonplace Book, and when he proposed to include it in his second edition of poems one of the academic mandarins of Edinburgh persuaded him not to sully its pages with such a picture of low life. So he never saw it in print, and was to write later: 'I kept no copy, indeed did not know that it was in existence.'

Burns and Gavin Hamilton at an alehouse in Mauchline.
Engraving by J. Rogers, from Allan Cunningham: Pictures and
Portraits of the Life and Land of Robert Burns, *1840.*

Chambers published Richmond's description of what occurred. 'After witnessing much jollity amongst a company who by day appeared as miserable beggars, the three young men came away, Burns professing to have been greatly amused with the scene, but particularly with the gleesome behaviour of an old maimed soldier. In the course of a few days he recited a part of the poem to Richmond, who informed me that, to the best of his recollection, it contained in its original complete form songs by a sweep and a sailor, which did not afterwards appear.' We may be thankful that the rest remains, for it is amongst the most original and precious of Robert's masterpieces. Here, as those Burns scholars, Henley and Henderson, expressed it, is 'humanity caught in the act'. Here the centre of the stage is given to people whom society has elbowed into the gutter, from where they thumb their noses at its conventions and its beliefs. They live in squalor, cheat and swear and become drunk, yet they enjoy companionship and uninhibited merriment and face their lot with courage. The sequence of poems – perhaps it should be called a song cycle – ends with the anarchist's affirmation:

> See the smoking bowl before us,
> Mark our jovial, ragged ring!
> Round and round take up the Chorus,
> And in raptures let us sing –
>> A fig for those by law protected!
>> LIBERTY's a glorious feast!
>> Courts for Cowards were erected,
>> Churches built to please the PRIEST.

The other poem of this season of spate in the inspired output of Robert Burns that stands apart as having no equal in the nation's literature is *Holy Willie's Prayer*. In this case it is known to have been composed in 1785.

Burns was by no means fundamentally irreligious, but he could not stomach the strict Calvinist doctrine of Predestination, which taught that the chosen people of God have been singled out as the Elect before their birth, so that nobody can win salvation by good works or a blameless life. More moderate views prevailed in the cities, but this cheerless creed still held many rural areas in its grip – and still does. Dr Auld, to whom Robert brought his certificate of good conduct from the parish of Tarbolton when he moved to Mossgiel, was among the stern upholders of the Westminster Confession. Holy Willie, an old bachelor of Mauchline named William Fisher, appears to have been the most sanctimonious of his Elders.

At his instigation Gavin Hamilton was summoned before the Church Session of Mauchline in 1784, charged with 'habitual neglect of Church ordinances'. When he protested by letter, more specific offences were listed, absence from Church on two Sabbaths in December and three in January, neglect of worship in his home, setting out on a journey on the Sabbath. The final accusation was that his letter to the Church Session had been abusive. Hamilton appealed to the

'The best laid schemes o' Mice an' Men,
Gang aft agley.'
Burns, improbably dressed for the task, disturbing the mouse's
nest with his plough in an engraving by John Le Conte from a
painting by Gowley Steel.

'A Guid New-year I wish thee, Maggie!
Hae, there's a ripp to thy auld baggie'
From Allan Cunningham: Pictures and Portraits of the Life and
Land of Robert Burns, *1840.*

Presbytery of Ayr, which exonerated him. The holy men of Mauchline took the case to the Synod of Glasgow and Ayr, where Hamilton won again. He had been defended by Robert Aiken.

Robert Burns depicted Holy Willie at his prayers after this lamentable outcome. In a note to his poem he described the creature as 'much and justly famed for that polemical chattering which ends in tippling Orthodoxy, and for that Spiritualized Bawdry which refines to Liqorish Devotion'. But even this is nothing to what follows, perhaps the most brilliant and devastating satire ever penned. Its opening stanza has been quoted already. It would be sacrilege to use scissors on the rest.

Among the animal poems of this period is the famous one he composed in November 1785 after he had disturbed a mouse's nest with his plough.

> But Mousie, thou art no [thy-lane],   [alone]
> In proving *foresight* may be vain:
> The best laid schemes o' *Mice* an' *Men*,
>   Gang aft [agley],   [awry]
> An' lea'e us nought but grief an' pain,
>   For promis'd joy!
>
> *To a Mouse, On turning her up in her*
> *Nest, with the Plough,*
> *November, 1785.*

In the same year Burns composed another poem which teaches mankind to extend sympathy and compassion to animals. In this case Maggie the mare, unlike the mouse, has shared her life with a human, ever since she was given to a farmer as a wedding present from his father-in-law twenty-nine years earlier. Bringing Maggie her New Year gift of corn, he reminds her of the occasion.

> That *day*, ye pranc'd wi' muckle pride,
> When ye [bure hame] my bonie *Bride*:
>   [bore home]
> An' sweet an' gracefu' she did ride
>   Wi' maiden air!

Now that the two of them are old, the farmer recalls the ups and downs of their lives, expressing his appreciation for all the mare's loyalty and help.

> An' think na, my auld, trusty *Servan'*,
> That now perhaps thou's less deservin,
> An' thy *auld days* may end in starvin',
>   For my last [fow],   [measure]
> A [heapet *Stimpart*], I'll reserve ane
>   [feed of grain]
>   Laid by for you.
>
> *The Auld Farmer's New-year-morning*
> *Salutation to his Auld Mare,*
> *Maggie.*

Once again the bard moves the reader without being sentimental.

A far longer animal poem of this prolific year is the conversation of the Two Dogs. Here it is the friends of man who speak with human voices, one of them of a foreign breed owned by a rich laird.

> The [tither] was a *ploughman's collie*,   [other]
> A rhyming, ranting, raving billie,
> Wha for his friend an' comrade had him,
> And in his freaks had *Luath* ca'd him;
> After some dog in *Highlan Sang*,
> Was made lang syne, lord knows how lang.
>
> *The Twa Dogs. A Tale.*

Not so long, in the bogus epic of MacPherson that Burns had read, in which 'swift-footed Luath' (which in Gaelic means swift) appears as the hound of Cuchullin. Cú Chulainn was himself the hero of an Irish Gaelic prose saga written down about a thousand years earlier, though far older in its subject matter. Burns was not to know that, nor how MacPherson had made use of the incidents in it that had trickled into the Scottish Gaelic folk repertoire. But this is worth considering, although it is irrelevant to the theme of Burns's poem, because it shows how he might have integrated the genuine Gaelic tradition in his writings if he had not remained in total ignorance of it.

Caesar, the wealthy man's dog, sees how the poor are treated at the Laird's court, and supposes their lives must be miserable. Luath reassures him that, on the contrary, they enjoy many kinds of happiness that money cannot buy, although

> They'll talk o' *patronage* an' *priests*,
> Wi' kindling fury i' their breasts

This was a reference to the privilege that landlords possessed to nominate a Minister, as patrons of the

The Twa Dogs.
'*Poor* tenant-bodies, *scant o' cash,*
How they maun thole a factor's *snash;*
He'll stamp an' threaten, curse an' swear,
He'll apprehend *them*, pound *their gear*'
From Allan Cunningham: Pictures and Portraits of the Life and
Land of Robert Burns.

parish. Lay patronage had been restored to the Church of Scotland, in defiance of an article of the Treaty of Union of 1707, some decades before the birth of Burns. It remained a source of social discord throughout his lifetime, and ultimately contributed to the Disruption of 1843 which created the Free Church of Scotland as a separate institution in which the power to call a Minister reverted to the parish congregation. John Galt's novels are particularly illuminating on the subject. The comments of Burns were more overtly political, influenced by a growing class prejudice.

This emerges in the rich man's dog's picture of the lives which the upper classes led. The money they ground from the poor was spent in dissipation, they wasted their patrimony abroad in revels from which they contracted venereal disease, they were bored by their idleness and could not find contentment in any of their amusements.

> There's some exceptions, man an' woman;
> But this is Gentry's life in common.

On the contrary, it is a preposterous travesty, excusable in a canine intelligence, totally unworthy of that of Robert Burns. It bears no resemblance to the picture of society to be found in the novels of Galt. It appears rather as another of the bard's extravagances, like his

parsonages. Generally, the landlord was preferring a moderate Minister to one with the doctrinal views of a Holy Willie. If the rule of the clergy was severe, at least they were not swayed by Burns's kind of class consciousness. No less a man than Gavin Hamilton was hailed before the Church Session, which could hardly have occurred in England.

A second factor was the almost universal access to education, for which the Presbyterian Church deserves such a large share of the credit. This had been one of the dreams of John Knox, though its implementation had been delayed until after the revolution of 1688 which placed the Calvinist William of Orange on the throne. By the time of Burns a barefoot shepherd's son from the Borders could walk to Edinburgh university with a bag of meal on his back. This university was run by the city fathers of the capital, whose liberal policies turned it into the most distinguished in Europe, in many fields of learning. The English gentry enrolled among Scottish peasants here, excluded from Oxford and Cambridge by the religious tests at those universities. In the far north, Highlanders without means could make the long trudge to the university of Aberdeen. Burns himself experienced the lack of class exclusiveness in the school at Ayr when he went there to study with John Murdoch. Children of the well-heeled gentry lent him books and helped him in his studies, and it was only later that he thought to remark on 'the immense distance between them and their ragged playmates'.

Then there was Freemasonry, which exercised perhaps a more levelling, kindly influence here than anywhere else in Europe. Brother Burns, Master Depute of his lodge, would not have been regarded as socially inferior by Brother Mackenzie because he was a physician or by Brother Hamilton who was a lawyer, whereas the bard was a farmer. As to that, Burns possessed a near relative who was a lawyer also. Hamilton might be his landlord and he a tenant, but this was a respectable status that entitled him to be called Rob Mossgiel. It is doubtful whether any of his better-placed friends thought in such terms in any case, though some biographers of Burns have done so.

The eccentricity of Rob Mossgiel's social attitude is revealed by comparing him with his *alter ego* Rob Donn, born forty-five years before him on the bottom rung of the ladder of his clan hierarchy. Rob Donn did not even enjoy the benefit of literacy or a formal education, yet he showed no inferiority complex as he mixed with the gentry and clergy, doctors, teachers and lawyers, handing out praise and blame as he saw fit. When he suffered for his independence of mind and

pretence of habitual drunkenness and pose as a rake.

The society of the Scottish Lowlands at this time was in fact amongst the most egalitarian in Europe. There was class stratification here as elsewhere, but it was eased by circumstances that were peculiar to that country. In the first place, the Presbyterian National Church was far more egalitarian in its structure than the Episcopal Church of England, and the re-introduction of patronage could do little to undermine this. Even when the lay patron imposed his nominee on a resentful congregation, he was likely to be someone very different from the younger sons of the aristocracy who were accommodated in the rich livings of English

behaviour, as he did on occasion, he remarked cheerfully that others who had farther to fall sometimes tripped on the threshold of authority. He was relatively fortunate.

> For although I should happen to stumble,
> It isn't far from my chin to the ground.
> *Translation by Ian Grimble.*

He was referring to his status, as much as his stature. Rob Donn also attacked fundamentalist doctrine, lashed unworthy Ministers, castigated oppressive landlords and condemned hypocrisy in high and low. But he did so in specific terms, never in class-conscious generalizations. He did not condemn the rich for dissipations which he celebrated in the behaviour of the poor, as Burns did in *The Jolly Beggars* and *The Twa Dogs*. Rob Donn represents the norm of the age in which he lived, Burns an aberration.

Why this should be so is a question for everyone's personal judgment. Burns was motivated by a deep compassion for the unfortunate, man and beast. His own life had acquainted him with misfortune early and endowed him with the courage to bear it. The very fact that he was not born in Rob Donn's lowly circumstances, yet reduced to a level below his family's proper status, may have contributed to his inferiority-complex, and his intellectual superiority may have exacerbated it. For the rest, it is surely significant that he chose to spend such a high proportion of his leisure time at a social level that offered sustenance to his sexual, rather than his mental, appetite.

He had a perfect right to do so. But Gavin Hamilton could not be accused of snobbery because he did not join his teen-age clerk John Richmond, the young linen draper James Smith and 'ranting roving Robin' in their ploys. Yet all his life Burns asserted a right to affront the conventions of respectable people as he chose, while he was quick to take offence when they expressed their disapproval. He was apt to attribute to class prejudice what was nothing of the sort, and say so with a venom that has made him the darling of promotors of class conflict.

The ultimate paradox, from which his greatest as well as his unworthiest utterances were fashioned, was this. The spell-binding talker, the good companion with such a sympathetic heart, was in himself introspective and self-doubting. His bouts of exuberance alternated with morbid moods of anxiety, increasingly aggravated by his 'hypochondria' as the years passed. Again and again he confessed as much, even to the mouse whose nest he had disturbed with his plough.

> Still, thou art blest compar'd wi' *me*!
> The *present* only toucheth thee:
> But Och! I *backward* cast my e'e,
>   On prospects drear!
> And *forward*, tho' I canna *see*,
>   I *guess* an' *fear*!

Manic depressives are apt to resort to the tonic of convivial habits, as Burns did, probably with a great deal less abandon than he pretended. But they sufficed to arouse prejudice in the little society of Mauchline parish, not least in that respectable and God-fearing master mason, James Armour. He cannot possibly be accused of snobbery in his attitude to Rob Mossgiel. He had eleven children to provide for, and the young tenant farmer so well endowed with intelligence and friends would have been a most eligible suitor for his daughter Jean but for the reputation his behaviour had earned him. As it was, James Armour would have none of him, and this was to precipitate the crisis of the bard's life.

Tarbolton, where Burns was inducted as a Freemason in July 1781. Procession of the St James Lodge. Engraving by D. O. Hill in Wilson and Chambers, The Land of Burns, *1840.*

Chapter 3

ROBERT FIRST ENCOUNTERED Jean Armour sometime in 1784, long before Elizabeth Paton bore him his first baby in May 1785. Jean was eighteen years old at that time, her hair a cluster of dark ringlets framing large, widely-spaced eyes above prominent cheek-bones. Her only portrait was painted in her widowhood, when her mouth had tightened, but it preserves a face that must have been beautiful, as well as a steady, unabashed outlook on life. Jean was said to have possessed a fine figure as well.

How soon Robert possessed Jean, whether she replaced Paton in his bed, or they took turn and turn about for a space, cannot be determined. But by January 1785 he was writing to David Sillar in one of his verse epistles:

> This life has joys for you and I;
> And joys that riches ne'er could buy;
>   And joys the very best.
> There's a' the *Pleasures o' the Heart*,
>   The *Lover* and the Frien';
> You have your MEG, your dearest part,
>   And I my darling JEAN!
> It warms me, it charms me,
> To mention but her *name*!
> It heats me, it [beets] me   [kindles]
> And sets me a' on flame!
>
> *Epistle to Davie, a Brother Poet.*

It would be surprising if the author of those words were not already enjoying what, to him, were 'joys the very best'.

When Robert's mother learnt of Paton's pregnancy, she urged her son to marry the girl, but Gilbert and his sisters were opposed to this. The bard's inclinations may be guessed. But he boasted to his friend John Rankine that he would make Paton pay in bed for the guinea fine he would incur when she bore him a bastard, even though his affections were now centred on Jean Armour. It does not display him in an attractive light.

> As soon's the [clockin-time] is by,   [hatching]
> An' the [wee powts] begun to cry,   [pullets]
> L – d, I 'se hae sportin by an' by,
> For my [gowd] guinea;   [gold]
>
> *Epistle to J.R., Enclosing some Poems.*

Elizabeth Paton accepted him on his own terms, as so many other girls were to do, and disappeared from the scene without complaint, leaving her daughter to be reared by Agnes Burness at Mossgiel.

Jean was the beneficiary of Robert's response to the outcome of his Paton affair, or so she must have believed, and so he appears to have intended at this time. He wrote in September 1785, before any question of Jean's pregnancy could have influenced his attitude: 'to have a woman to lie with when one pleases, without running any risk of the cursed expence of bastards and all the other concomitants of that species of smuggling – these are solid views of matrimony'. Not very romantic ones, however; not in the least in the spirit of the epistle to David Siller that he had composed in the previous January. But the author of some of the most tender and lofty love lyrics in the English language was apt to descend to earth with a thud in his prose.

When the New Year of 1786 arrived, the argument in favour of marriage had gained weight with Jean's condition. The mystery to which there is no certain answer, though many hypotheses, is what prompted Burns, instead of marrying Jean, to descend to the most elaborate subterfuges to evade the status of a married man. Jean's father, it is true, would have none of him as a son-in-law, and packed his pregnant daughter off to relatives in Paisley. But under the law of Scotland Burns could claim that Jean was in fact his wife by 'use and wont', of which her pregnancy provided incontestable proof. There was no need for him to give her a written declaration, though he did this. The question is, who advised him to do this, and with what motive. It has been surmised that the lawyer Gavin Hamilton drew it up for him: certainly it was his

Sic herdum, derdum ← ← sue din,
The minstrels did never blin,
Wi' he o'er her & she o'er him
wi michle mirth and glee.

Dance in a Barn. Pen and wash drawing by David Allan
(1744–1796).

other legal friend Robert Aiken from Ayr who visited the Armours and advised Jean's father to cut the signatures out of the bard's declaration. Superfluous as the document had been in the first place, as any lawyer would have known, it would have been far simpler to throw it in the fire, unless the mutilated version could serve a legal purpose, as evidence.

The essential fact it could demonstrate was that Burns had made an honourable proposal of marriage, which had been formally rejected. This the bard emphasised from now on, in a histrionic manner, as though he were collecting witnesses for his submission that he was now legally a bachelor, rather than a married man by use and wont. In April he wrote to Hamilton accepting the loss of Jean as final, and blaming both her and Aiken for the outcome. This letter might provide another piece of material evidence. 'Old Mr Armour prevailed with him [Aiken] to mutilate that unlucky paper yesterday. Would you believe it? Though I had not a hope, nor a wish, to make her mine after her damnable conduct, yet when he told me the names were cut out of the paper my heart died within me, and cut my very veins with the news.' In case Armour should destroy the paper, Burns had written at once to the other lawyer in the case, providing corroboratory evidence.

As for Jean, waiting in Paisley to discover whether her lover would find a means of rescuing her, as he could so easily have done, he had only this to say. 'Perdition seize her falsehood and perfidious perfidy! But God bless and forgive my poor, once-dear, misguided girl. She is ill-advised.' That at least appears to have been true.

Burns dramatized his situation in a remarkable letter that he sent to John Arnot, son of a former factor to the Earl of Loudoun. In it, the miserable Jean was sacrificed on the altar of art. 'I had long had a wishing eye to that inestimable blessing, a wife. My mouth watered deliciously to see a young fellow, after a few idle, commonplace stories from a gentleman in black, strip and go to bed with a young girl, and no one durst say, black was his eye; while I, for doing just the same thing, only wanting that ceremony, am made a Sunday's laughing-stock and abused like a pickpocket.'

He went on to claim that he had made Jean pregnant with the deliberate intention of claiming her as his wife under Scots Law, as he could have done but did not. 'I was well aware though, that if my ill-starred fortune got the least hint of my connubial wish, my schemes would go for nothing. To prevent this, I determined to take my measures with such thought and forethought, such a caution and precaution, that all the malignant planets in the hemisphere should be unable to blight my designs. Not content with, to use the words of the

The carter's lunch. Pen and ink drawing by James Howe.

Country folk in 18th-century Scotland. Milking, a pencil
drawing by Walter Geikie.

celebrated Westminster Divines, "The outward and ordinary means", I left no *stone* unturned; sounded every unfathomed *depth*; stopped up every *hole* and bore of an objection.

'But how shall I tell it? Notwithstanding all this turning of stones, stopping of bores etc., whilst I with secret pleasure marked my project *swelling* to a proper crisis, and was singing Te Deum in my own fancy; or, to change the metaphor, whilst I was vigorously pressing on the siege; had carried the counter-scarp, and made a practicable breach behind the curtain in the gorge of the very principal bastion; nay, having mastered the covered way, I had found means to slip in a choice detachment into the very citadel; while I had nothing less in view than displaying my victorious banners on the top of the walls – Heaven and Earth, must I remember? – my damned Star wheeled about to the zenith, by whose baleful rays Fortune took the alarm, and pouring in her forces on all quarters, front, flank and rear, I was utterly routed, my baggage lost, my military chest in the hands of the enemy; and your poor devil of a humble servant, commander in chief forsooth, was obliged to scamper away without either arms or honours of war, except his bare bayonet and cartridge-pouch; nor in all probability had he escaped even with them, had he not made a shift to hide them under the lap of his military cloak.'

Nothing that Burns did or wrote at this time can be explained entirely unless he was seeking to escape from a criminal charge of bigamy. Nor is the part of Aiken the lawyer comprehensible – or of Hamilton either – unless they were abetting him in the stratagem by which he succeeded in establishing his status as a bachelor so far as Jean Armour was concerned. The other girl in the case was Mary Campbell, and it is noteworthy that she was the only girl in his entire life about whom he was both secretive and mendacious. The question is when, if at all, did she acquire a property in his bayonet and cartridge pouch which entitled her, in the eyes of her parents, to consider herself his wife by use and wont.

Robert's family remained equally tight-lipped about Mary, even after the bard's death. But his mother and sister Isabella then deposed that he had consorted with her only after he had been 'deserted' by Jean Armour. Their exact dating is noteworthy. Jean was sent to Paisley in March and Mary died in October, possibly in child-birth, or soon after she had borne a child which died also. If Burns did not associate with her until after Jean had left him, then he could not have been responsible for this, and might escape a charge of bigamy.

But Mary Campbell came to Gavin Hamilton's home in Mauchline as a nursemaid to his son Alexander, who was born on 13 July 1785. So Burns would have had ample opportunity to make her acquaintance earlier. She was designated a Highlander, not because she lived on top of a mountain, but as a Gaelic speaker. She lived with her parents near Dunoon in Cowel, on the west side of the Firth of Clyde, then at Campbeltown on the Mull of Kintyre, and latterly in Greenock. Gaelic is no longer spoken generally in any of these places today, but it was the language of all three until long after Mary's time. On the other hand, people received no formal education in Gaelic, even up to the 20th century. Mary would have been taught to read and write English, and was evidently able to understand the letters Burns wrote her in this language.

Among the few hard facts about their relationship that have survived the systematic cover-up is Burns's promise of marriage. The material evidence consists of a Bible in two volumes, preserved today in the Ayr monument. Whether or not he gave it to her when she left Mauchline to return home on 14 May 1786, this Bible bears witness that he had plighted his troth to her. It also reveals that Mary's family were as little pleased as the Armours when they saw Robert's declaration to Jean. One volume was inscribed with Mary's name, the other with Robert's, and both have been partially erased. But the Bible contains Robert's mason's mark, and texts from Leviticus and Saint Matthew in his handwriting which condemn false swearing and non-performance of oaths. It has been suggested that the Campbell family could not bring themselves to destroy so valuable a property, and indeed it has proved to be of inestimable value. But in any case, such people did not treat the Word of God with disrespect. They did, however, display implacable hostility to Burns after Mary's death.

This has to be accounted for, like the attitude of the Armours. So do the eccentric, almost hysterical acts and words of Burns during this summer of 1786. His letter to John Arnot complaining of Jean Armour's removal to Paisley rises to a crescendo of desperation in which the predicament of the poor girl is totally forgotten. 'How I bore this can only be conceived. All powers of recital labour far, far behind. There is a pretty large portion of bedlam in the composition of a poet at any time; but on this occasion I was nine parts and nine-tenths out of ten stark, staring mad. At first, I was fixed in stuporific insensibility, silent, sullen, staring like Lot's wife be-saltified in the plains of Gomorrah. But my second paroxysm chiefly beggars description. The rifted ocean when returning suns dissolve the chains of winter, and loosening precipices of long accumulated ice tempest with hideous crash the foaming deep – images like these may give some faint shadow of what was the situation of my bosom.'

Allowing for his delight in self-dramatization, we may conclude that Burns was in considerable danger of some kind. As the letter progresses, Jean Armour disappears from the lurid scene. 'My chained faculties broke loose; my maddening passions, roused to a tenfold fury, bore over their banks with impetuous, resistless force, carrying every check and principle before them. Counsel was an unheeded call to the passing hurricane; Reason a feebly-screaming elk in the vortex of Moskoestroem; and Religion a struggling beaver

Gavin Hamilton (1751–1805). Drawn by Otto Leyde from an original painting. Scottish National Portrait Gallery, Edinburgh.

down the roarings of Niagara. I reprobated the first moment of my existence; execrated Adam's folly-infatuated wish for that goodly-looking, but poison-breathing gift, which had ruined him and undone me; and called on the womb of uncreated night to close over me and all my sorrows.'

Robert Burns, in fact, was in a fix, and it brought out the canny side of his character as well as the poetic one. He took the practical steps which anyone of sense might do if he stood in danger of arrest on a criminal charge of bigamy. His pledge to Mary Campbell presumably remained a secret in Mauchline, the attitude of her parents uncertain. But the imbroglio with Jean Armour was public knowledge. The Armours could have held him to his promise to marry the girl but instead they had repudiated him. While Burns trumpeted his tragedy into every ear, he turned it to his salvation by applying for a bachelor's certificate from his parish Minister. That would release him from a charge of bigamy if Mary Campbell's parents were to adopt a different attitude.

At the same time he made arrangements to leave the country. As he told John Arnot: 'Already the holy beagles, the houghmagandie [fornication] pack, begin to snuff the scent, and I expect every moment to see them cast off, and hear them after me in full cry. But as I am an old fox, I shall give them dodging and doubling for it; and by and by I intend to earth among the mountains of Jamaica.' On the contrary, he would not have needed to flee abroad from a charge of fornication, and he stepped forward openly with a confession of it, as the grounds for obtaining his bachelor's certificate. If the Church decreed that he had committed fornication, then he could not have been Jean's husband by use and wont. In this case he could not have committed bigamy.

He continued to conduct his own public relations campaign with specious eloquence. Among his Mauchline friends was David Brice, who had gone to Glasgow as a shoemaker. Burns wrote to him in June: 'Poor, ill-advised, ungrateful Armour came home on Friday last. You have heard all the particulars of that affair; and a black affair it is. What she thinks of her conduct now, I don't know. One thing I know, she has made me completely miserable. Never man loved, or rather adored, a woman more than I did her: and, to confess a truth between you and me, I do still love her to distraction after all, though I won't tell her so though I see her, which I won't do.' Presumably he had told Mary Campbell instead, when he plighted his troth to her a few weeks earlier.

Compliant as Jean was to remain all her life in her

devotion to the bard, she sent a confession to the Church Session on 18 June. 'I am heartily sorry that I have given and must give your Session trouble on my account. I acknowledge that I am with child, and Robert Burns in Mossgiel is the father. I am, with great respect, your humble servant.' A week later Robert appeared before the Church Session in person to admit the truth of her allegation. Holy Willie may well have savoured his humiliation, not realising how he was escaping a worse fate. Old Dr Auld may well have treated him with consideration. Although he was a Minister of the stern Calvinist school, Burns showed him a respect that he did not accord lightly to such people.

Certainly Robert was allowed to stand in his pew in church, rather than beside Jean in the place of repentance, on the three successive Sabbaths when their sins were expounded from the pulpit. As he wrote to David Brice, 'I have already appeared publicly in Church, and was indulged in the liberty of standing in my own seat. I do this to get a certificate as a bachelor, which Mr Auld has promised me. I am now fixed to go for the West Indies in October.' He had begun making his plans to do this in April, and during this year he protested that he was doing it in order to earn the means for Mary Campbell's support, to whom he was betrothed.

> For her I'll dare the billow's roar;
> For her I'll trace a distant shore;
> That Indian wealth may lustre throw
> Around my Highland lassie O.
>
> She has my heart, she has my hand,
> By secret troth and honour's band.
> Till the mortal stroke shall lay me low
> I'm thine, my Highland lassie O.
>
> *Highland Lassie O.*

A poem that did not appear in print until 1792 went further than this in suggesting that Robert invited Mary to sail to Jamaica with him.

> Will ye go to the Indies, my Mary,
> And leave auld Scotia's shore;
> Will you go to the Indies, my Mary,
> Across th' Atlantic roar?
> We hae plighted our truth, my Mary,
> In mutual affection to join:
> And curst be the cause that shall part us,
> The hour and the moment of time!!!
>
> *Song*, to the tune,
> *Ewe bughts Marion.*

Not a word of Mary in all those letters in which Robert broadcast Jean's betrayal of him, his despair, his undying love for her. Her exclusion must have been very deliberate. But Burns could substitute Jean for Mary in one of his poems of farewell. It is addressed to his mother and family, then turns to James Smith the young linen draper.

> Adieu too, to you too,
> My Smith, my bosom frien';
> When kindly you mind me,
> O then befriend my Jean!
> What bursting anguish tears my heart;
> From thee, my Jeany, must I part!
> Thou, weeping, answ'rest – 'No!'
> Alas! Misfortune stares my face,
> And points to ruin and disgrace,
> I for thy sake must go!
>
> *The Farewell.*

Neither Mary nor her parents could have been very pleased if they had read that.

As for ruin and disgrace, Robert found himself confronting a new danger in July, while he was making his peace with the Church, and arranging to leave the country. James Armour obtained a writ against him on the grounds that he planned to flee from his financial obligations to Jean. Robert learnt of it in time to execute a deed conveying all his property to his brother Gilbert on 22 July, before the writ could be served, which he avoided by going into hiding. In this he acted as astutely as he so often did in an emergency. But the episode cast him into another of his moods of despondency, from which he found release by writing to his friend John Richmond, now a clerk in an Edinburgh advocate's firm. Once again, Jean is the scapegoat, although it appears to have been she who sent Burns timely warning of what her father intended.

'My hour is come. You and I will never meet in Britain more. I have orders within three weeks at farthest to repair aboard the *Nancy*, Captain Smith, from Clyde to Jamaica, and to call at Antigua. This, except to our friend Smith, whom God long preserve, is a secret about Mauchline. Would you believe it? Armour has got a warrant to throw me in jail till I find security for an enormous sum. This they keep an entire secret, but I got it by a channel they little dream of, and I am wandering from one friend's house to another, and like a true son of the Gospel "have nowhere to lay my head". I know you will pour an execration on her head, but spare the poor, ill-advised girl for my sake; though may all the Furies that rend the injured, enraged lover's bosom await the old harridan, her mother, until her latest hour.' Fortunately Richmond disobeyed Burns's instruction, 'For Heaven's sake burn this letter.'

As for the ruin with which Robert felt himself to be threatened, it would not be surprising if the affairs of Mossgiel had been plunged into some disarray during this year in which the head of the house had been pursuing such an erratic course. Moody at the best of times, he must have been trying to live with, although his letters contain no expression of concern for the family who were struggling to run the farm during his tantrums. Now he was missing from his home altogether, and planning to leave the country in three weeks at the latest.

But the previous April, while Jean was in Paisley

Kilmarnock, where the first edition of Burns's poetry was printed. Engraving by D. O. Hill for Wilson and Chambers: The Land of Burns, 1840.

and he was consoling himself with Mary, he had taken another practical step besides his arrangements to emigrate. He had approached a printer in Kilmarnock with a view to having his poetry published. In the prospectus that Burns submitted to him, he declared: 'As the Author has not the most distant *Mercenary* view in Publishing, as soon as so many Subscribers appear as will defray the *necessary* Expence, the Work will be sent to the Press.'

It has been suggested that he was being less than honest in disclaiming any financial motive. Certainly Burns could strike an attitude, especially when his pride was involved. Of course he must have hoped that his venture would prove profitable. Yet we must believe him when he said that his overriding motive was to leave behind a memento of himself in his native land when he emigrated, hoping it would be one that brought him credit in the judgment of his fellow countrymen. Some have doubted whether he ever seriously intended to go to Jamaica. Others will agree that his words in a letter he wrote to Dr John Moore in 1787 reveals his true state of mind in both these matters.

''Twas a delicious idea that I would be called a clever fellow, even though it should never reach my ears, a poor Negro-driver, or perhaps a victim to that inhospitable clime gone to the world of Spirits.' Here his introspective nature most honestly confessed. 'To know myself had been all along my constant study. I weighed myself alone; I balanced myself with others. I watched every means of information how much ground I occupied both as a Man and as a Poet. I studied assiduously Nature's DESIGN where she seemed to have intended the various LIGHTS and SHADES in my character. I was pretty sure my poems would meet with some applause; but at the worst, the roar of the Atlantic would deafen the voice of Censure, and the novelty of West-Indian scenes make me forget Neglect.'

The subscriptions were satisfactory; the selection of poems was sent to Kilmarnock in June. They were in the press when James Armour obtained his writ against the author in the following month. Robert's deed of trust in favour of his brother Gilbert handed

Dr John Moore (1729–1802), physician and author of the influential novel Zeluco, *to whom Burns wrote his most revealing autobiographical letter. From the portrait by Sir Thomas Lawrence.*

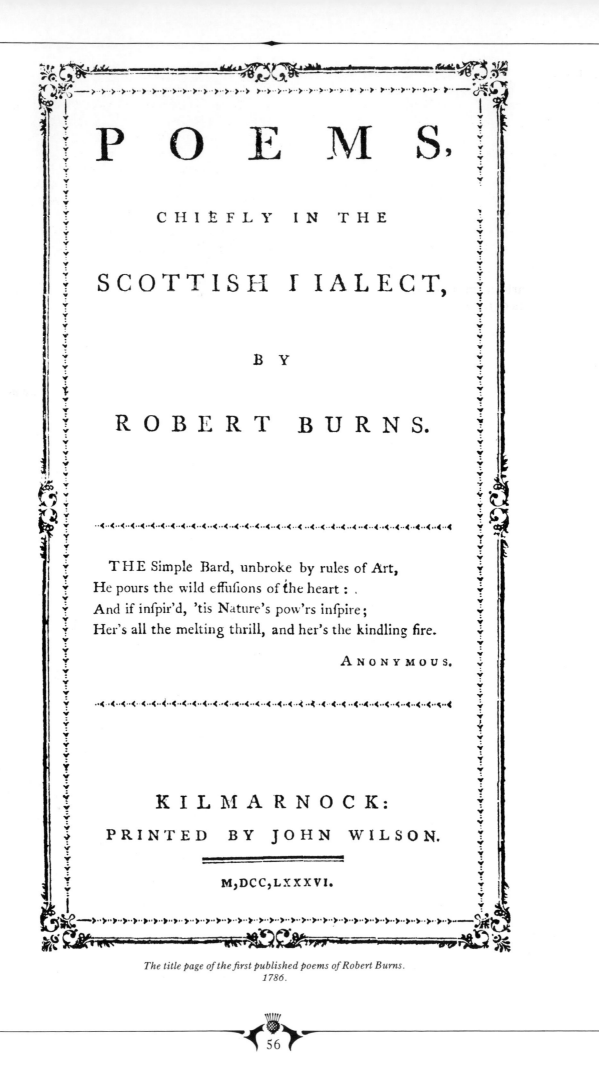

POEMS,

CHIEFLY IN THE

SCOTTISH DIALECT,

BY

ROBERT BURNS.

THE Simple Bard, unbroke by rules of Art,
He pours the wild effusions of the heart:
And if infpir'd, 'tis Nature's pow'rs infpire;
Her's all the melting thrill, and her's the kindling fire.

ANONYMOUS.

KILMARNOCK:
PRINTED BY JOHN WILSON.

M,DCC,LXXXVI.

The title page of the first published poems of Robert Burns.
1786.

him, in addition to his other assets, 'the profits that may arise from the publication of my poems presently in the press'. The copyright of Robert's poems was to be used by Gilbert for the maintenance of Elizabeth Paton's daughter.

On 31 July 1786 was published *Poems, Chiefly in the Scottish Dialect*. It was a small event in a provincial town, at a time when news travelled at the speed of a horse. Burns assuaged his personal worries and an author's anxiety over the reception of his first book in convivial, farewell visits to his friends. Tarbolton Lodge gave an affectionate send-off to their former Master Depute.

> Adieu! A heart-warm, fond adieu!
> Dear brothers of the *mystic tye*!
> Ye favour'd, ye enlighten'd few,
> Companions of my social joy!
> Tho' I to foreign lands must hie,
> Pursuing Fortune's [slidd'ry ba']   [slippery ball]
> With melting heart, and brimful eye,
> I'll mind you still, tho' far awa'.
>
> Oft have I met your social band
> And spent the cheerful, festive night;
> Oft, honour'd with supreme command,
> Presided o'er the *Sons of light*:
> And by that *Hieroglyphic* bright,
> Which none but *Craftsmen* ever saw!
> Strong mem'ry on my heart shall write
> Those happy scenes when far awa'!
>
> *The Farewell. To the Brethren of St James's Lodge, Tarbolton.*

While he was preparing to board the *Nancy* at Greenock he met a married couple in Ayr who had just returned from Jamaica. They warned him against travelling to a port of that island which would involve him in a long and arduous journey to the plantation to which he was bound. They told him of another ship called the *Bell* which would be sailing for Kingston in Jamaica in September. Its skipper was a friend of Gavin Hamilton's named Captain Cathcart. So Burns returned to Mossgiel instead of riding on to Greenock.

Once again we are faced with the mystery of Mary Campbell. Had Burns continued to Greenock he would presumably have said farewell to her there before he sailed, even if he had not taken her with him. She had gone home to stay with her parents in Campbeltown where, in the event, she remained unemployed until she went to stay in Greenock in October. Her parents' hatred of Burns, if possible even more virulent than that of the Armours, requires an explanation, and it must be found in the events of this summer. None fits all the known facts except a supposition that by now Mary was pregnant by Burns, and her parents knew it. It may be that they, unlike the Armours, expected him to marry the girl. Suffice it to say, he changed his mind about going to Greenock. Since the Campbells destroyed all his letters and Burns

kept his mouth shut, the mystery remains insoluble.

On 3 September Jean Armour's brother came to Mossgiel with the news that his sister had given birth to twins. This was when Robert sent his bawdy version of *Green grow the rushes O* to John Richmond with the news. 'Wish me luck, dear Richmond. Armour has just brought me a fine boy and girl at one throw. God bless the little dears.' Pride of parenthood as well as its responsibilities may have influenced his decision when he allowed the *Bell* to sail without him in September, for both weighed heavily with him. But a more powerful motive was soon added to this one.

Before Robert's return to Mossgiel, he had visited George Laurie, the Minister of Loudoun at Newmilns, who had already seen and admired his published poems and had sent a copy of them to Thomas Blacklock in Edinburgh. A blind Doctor of Divinity who had been reared in Annan, Blacklock published a volume of poems long before Robert's birth and was by this time one of the most respected literary critics of the capital. On 4 September he wrote an acknowledgment to Laurie, who forwarded his letter to Gavin Hamilton, who in turn showed it to Burns. If Burns did not wake up to find himself famous when his volume appeared from the press, as Byron was to do when *Childe Harold* was published, the delayed reaction could only have been more gratifying when it reached his ears.

'There is a pathos and delicacy in his serious poems,' wrote Blacklock, 'a vein of wit and humour in those of

Rev. George Laurie (1727–99), Minister of Loudoun, who played a crucial part in introducing the poetry of Burns to the literary world of Edinburgh. Engraving by W. F. Hall from a painting by W. Bonner.

Dr Thomas Blacklock (1721–1791). The blind Edinburgh poet to
whom Burns addressed his famous lines:
To make a happy fireside clime
To weans and wife,
That's the true Pathos *and* Sublime
Of human life.
Engraving by W. F. Holl.

Dr Hugh Blair (1718–1800). He was appointed to the new Chair
of Rhetoric at Edinburgh University in 1762, and in the
following year published his Dissertation, maintaining the
authenticity of MacPherson's Ossianic epics. Engraving by
I. Kay, 1798.

a more festive turn, which cannot be too much admired, nor too warmly approved; and I shall never open the book without feeling my astonishment renewed and increased.' Few have disagreed with that judgment since; on the other hand, not every poet of Burns' stature has received such instant acclaim. To crown it all, Blacklock reported the interest of Edinburgh's other arbiters of taste, including Dugald Stewart, who had recently been appointed Professor of Moral Philosophy at Edinburgh University.

'Mr Stewart, professor of morals in this university, had formerly read me three of the poems, and I had desired to get my name inserted among the subscribers: but whether this was done or not I could never learn. I have little intercourse with Dr Blair, but will take care to have the poems communicated to him by the intervention of some mutual friend.' Hugh Blair appears ridiculous today for his championship of the Ossianic epics of James MacPherson, whose authenticity he asserted although he probably did not even know how many letters there are in the Gaelic alphabet. But he could be expected to exercise a sounder judgment where English poetry was concerned, whether in dialect or not.

Blacklock concluded by remarking that the Kilmarnock edition of the poems was sold out. 'It were therefore much to be wished, for the sake of the young man, that a second edition, more numerous than the former, could immediately be printed; as it appears

certain that its intrinsic merit, and the exertion of the author's friends, might give it a more universal circulation than anything of the kind which has been published within my memory.'

Surely it was Blacklock, more than anyone, who saved the apostle of liberty, the champion of the equality of man, from becoming an overseer of slaves in Jamaica.

In October Burns dined with Dugald Stewart at his country house near Mauchline. Less than six years older than the twenty-seven-year-old poet, Stewart was a man of inspiring eloquence with an outstanding gift for stimulating the young men whom he taught, who were to include some of the most distinguished Scotsmen of the age. His nature was liberal, his views eclectic. He was the most gifted person yet of a kind whose society Robert Burns enjoyed already, professional men older than himself such as Laurie the moderate Minister, Hamilton the lawyer and Mackenzie the physician. Accustomed to such company, Burns evidently scintillated at the table of Dugald Stewart, who rated his conversation as Dr Mackenzie had done already.

Stewart remarked to William Robertson, Principal of Edinburgh University, after he had also seen some of Burns' letters: 'Robert Burns's poems had, he acknowledged, surprised him; his prose compositions appeared even more wonderful; but the conversation was a marvel beyond all.' The diversity of those who testified to this is another marvel. Evidently Burns could adapt himself to all sorts and conditions of people with consummate art.

The Professor left a graphic description of the bard, which he dated back to this first meeting at his home near Mauchline. 'His manners were then, as they continued ever afterwards, simple, manly and independent; strongly expressive of conscious genius and worth; but without anything that indicated forwardness, arrogance or vanity. He took his share in the conversation, but not more than belonged to him, and listened with apparant attention and deference, on subjects where his want of education deprived him of the means of information.' The portrait is candid enough to include a comment, though less astringent than that of David Sillar, on the bard's biting tongue. 'If there had been a little more of gentleness and accommodation in his temper, he would, I think, have been still more interesting.' But perhaps not his poetry, any more than that of Rob Donn, both of which contain such masterpieces of satire.

Burns' summer of mental torment might have flowed into an autumn of euphoria. He had obtained the vital bachelor's certificate in August. In September

Jean Armour had been delivered safely of the twins named Robert and Jean and they were left in the care of his mother. Only a few weeks later he found himself transformed from a local celebrity into a national poet. Yet he remained in a state of anguish, all the more tortured because he could not find relief, as he generally did, by telling the whole story (or at least, his side of it) to a friend. The confessional was ever one of the most therapeutic remedies for the emotional ailments of Burns. On this occasion, for whatever reason, it was closed to him, and he could only describe himself as a criminal, without naming his crime. He wrote to Robert Aiken the lawyer.

'I have for some time been pining under secret wretchedness from causes which you pretty well know – the pang of disappointment, the sting of pride, with some wandering stabs of remorse, which never fail to

---

Dugald Stewart (1753–1828), Professor of Moral Philosophy at Edinburgh University when Burns went to the capital. From the painting of Stewart with his family by Alexander Naysmith in a private collection.

settle on my vitals like vultures, when attention is not called away by the calls of society, or the vagaries of the Muse. Even in the hour of social mirth, my gaiety is the madness of an intoxicated criminal under the hands of the executioner.'

The only conceivable cause for his continuing anxiety is Mary Campbell. Whether or not she would have gone from Campbeltown to Greenock in September to meet him, had he persisted in his plan to take ship there, she made the journey in October instead. The reason why she should have done this is as mysterious as the cause of her remaining at home without working during the preceding months, unless she was pregnant. Whether or not she stayed with a relative called Peter MacPherson, as Jean Armour had gone to stay with kinsfolk in Paisley, it was MacPherson who buried her in his lair in the old Greenock West Churchyard when she died soon after her arrival. Burns's youngest sister was to relate that a letter was delivered at Mossgiel late in October, which he took to the light of a window to read. Deeply upset, he then left the room without a word to anyone and disappeared from his home. Nobody knows who wrote that letter.

The bard's most comprehensive and universally respected biographer, the American scholar Dr Franklyn Snyder, left no doubt of his belief that Mary became pregnant by Burns about a month after Jean Armour did, and that he made them both a declaration of marriage, unnecessary in each case under Scots Law. Hence his terror, his eagerness to repudiate Jean and obtain a bachelor's certificate, the definite arrange-ments he made to leave the country. Mary's death, whether or not in childbirth, ought to have taken an immense weight of anxiety off his shoulders. But it left him with feelings of remorse such as he never displayed over his treatment of any other woman, although this was, on more than one occasion, such as a misogynist could hardly have devised. They are to be explained in Dr Snyder's opinion only by the fact that Mary Campbell was the one girl to have died as a result of his sexual attentions.

Three years later, Burns delivered himself of a rather different interpretation of what had occurred, as he had such a talent for doing in verse.

Thou lingering star with lessening ray
That lovest to greet the early morn,
Again thou usherest in the day
My Mary from my soul was torn –
O Mary! dear departed Shade!
Where is thy place of blissful rest?
Seest thou thy Lover lowly laid?
Hearest thou the groans that rend his breast?

That sacred hour can I forget,
Can I forget the hallowed grove,
Where by the winding Ayr we met,
To live one day of Parting Love?
Eternity can not efface
Those records of dear transports past;
Thy image at our last embrace,
Ah, little thought we 'twas our last!

A Song, to the tune, *Captain Cook's death.*

By 1789 Robert Burns was polishing up his authorized version of the Mary Campbell affair for the enlightenment of posterity. In 1794 he added this further explanation. 'My Highland Lassie was a warmhearted, charming young creature as ever blessed a man with generous love. After a pretty long tract of the most ardent reciprocal attachment, we met by appointment, on the second Sunday in May, in a sequestered spot by the banks of Ayr, where we spent the day in taking farewell, before she should embark for the West Highlands to arrange matters among her friends for our projected change of life.' A pretty long tract of time sounds a great deal longer than the period between March, when Jean was sent to Paisley, and May when Robert and Mary parted. So much for his furious complaints at that time that it was his beloved Jean who had deserted him.

His explanation continues: 'At the close of Autumn following she crossed the sea to meet me at Greenock, where she had scarcely landed when she was seized with a malignant fever, which hurried my dear girl to the grave in a few days before I could even hear of her illness.' Such was the fantasy in which he had either come to believe himself, or at least to hope that the world would believe. It gave rise to the romantic legend that Mary was the one true love of his life, torn from him by death, although there is not a shred of evidence that Burns knew the meaning of constant love for a woman. However, this interpretation is made possible by Robert's total reticence on the subject of Mary, in the candid letters he wrote to his friends at the time of the imbroglio. Possible, but not likely. For however vehemently he repudiated Jean in those letters, he still protested his love for her.

We should spare a thought for the family of Rob Mossgiel in the aftermath of Mary Campbell's death. A month earlier he had been about to leave them; perhaps forever, since the mortality rate of Europeans in the West Indies was formidable. Now he was back in their midst, his emotional turmoil presumably subsiding. There was not even a fourth bastard to be accommodated in the lap of the long-suffering Agnes Burness. To crown their sense of relief, her son was suddenly celebrated.

November brought an Indian summer. 'We, Robert Burns, by virtue of a Warrant from Nature,' the bard proclaimed himself, 'Poet Laureate and Bard in Chief in and over the Districts of Kyle, Cunningham and Carrick of old extent . . .' On 15 November he wrote to Mrs Dunlop, 'I am thinking to go to Edinburgh in a week or two at farthest, to throw off a second impression of my book.'

Chapter 4

O F ALL THE ADMIRERS who stepped forward to help and encourage the bard, posterity owes the largest debt to Mrs Dunlop of Dunlop. Recently widowed, she was roused from her gloom by reading the Kilmarnock volume, in which *The Cottar's Saturday Night* pleased her best of all. She sent to Mossgiel for six copies of the book, and invited the author to visit her at Dunlop House, some fifteen miles distant. Burns could supply no more than five, which he sent with the comment: 'I am fully persuaded that there is not any class of Mankind so feelingly alive to the titillations of applause as the sons of Parnassus, nor is it easy to conceive how the heart of the poor bard dances with rapture, when those, whose character in life gives them a right to be polite Judges, honour him with their approbation.' This letter, which he wrote on 15 November 1786, is the first of 79 that have survived, the largest number he addressed to any single person and a priceless key to his thoughts and feelings for most of the remainder of his life.

Mrs Dunlop was the daughter of Sir Thomas Wallace, and allowed no one to remain in ignorance of her family connection with the patriot leader who had sacrificed his life to the cause of Scottish independence nearly 500 years earlier. She was almost thirty years older than Burns, which protected them both from his propensity for regarding women primarily as potential bed-fellows. He had already burnt his fingers with another member of the gentry when he composed his poem to Miss Wilhelmina Alexander of Ballochmyle, saying,

> O if she were a country Maid,
> And I the happy country Swain!
> Though shelt'red in the lowest shed
> That ever rose on Scotia's plain:
> Through weary Winter's wind and rain,
> With joy, with rapture I would toil,
> And nightly to my bosom strain
> The bonnie Lass o' Ballochmyle.
>
> *Song. On Miss W.A.*, to the tune, *Ettrick banks.*

A plain, respectable spinster of thirty, Miss Alexander may well have suspected that she was the victim of a cruel joke. At any rate she aired her displeasure to the extent of extracting an apology for the song that has given her immortality. In the November of Burns's first letter to Mrs Dunlop, he excused himself to Wilhelmina with the observation: 'Poets are such outré beings.'

Mrs Dunlop he accepted in the role she established for herself from the start, that of a maternal adviser, confidante and helper of young genius. She also aspired to the part of censor, when Burns would put her in her place, with more or less tact as the mood took him.

He did not call to visit her when he set out for Edinburgh on 27 November, on a pony borrowed from a farmer near Ochiltree. The journey took him two days, during which he was entertained hospitably wherever he alighted, and especially at Biggar where he spent the night. His diseased constitution, which so tragically belied his robust appearance, had succumbed to the strain by the time he reached the capital. John Richmond, Gavin Hamilton's former clerk in Mauchline, was working here by this time and conducted Burns to the lodgings they were to share. It stood among the towering buildings of the old town and here Burns paid three shillings a week to the landlady for a half of Richmond's bed. On a higher floor, prostitutes plied their trade.

It was during his bout of illness in these surroundings, so different from Mossgiel, that he wrote to Sir John Whitefoord on 1 December in a manner that reflects the symptoms of his 'hypochondriacs'. Dr Mackenzie in Mauchline, his father's physician and his own, had introduced him to this well-wisher, one of many who had done nothing to earn such a shaft as Burns directed at him when he assured Whitefoord that he was not 'the needy, sharping author, fastening on those in upper life, who honour him with a little notice of him and his work'. It is not as though Burns acted on those words. He did not hesitate to present the

Mrs Dunlop of Dunlop (1730–1815). Posterity owes her a debt for extracting more letters from Burns than any of his other correspondents. Portrait by an unknown artist in the Scottish National Portrait Galley, Edinburgh.

introduction, which an admirer had given him, to the Earl of Glencairn, a nobleman who was to honour him with a great deal more than a little notice. Within a week of the letter to Whitefoord, he was writing to Gavin Hamilton in altogether higher spirits, telling him of the attentions of Glencairn and the 11th Earl of Buchan's brother, Henry Erskine.

'I am in a fair way of becoming as eminent as Thomas à Kempis or John Bunyan; and you may expect henceforth to see my birthday inserted among the wonderful events, in the Poor Robin's and Aberdeen Almanacks, along with the Black Monday, and the battle of Bothwell bridge. My Lord Glencairn and the Dean of Faculty, Mr H. Erskine, have taken me under their wing, and by all probability I shall soon be the tenth worthy, and the eighth Wise Man, of the World.' A week later he was writing to John Ballantine, the banker of Ayr who had assisted him in the selection of his poems for the Kilmarnock edition, 'my avowed Patrons and Patronesses are the Duchess of Gordon, the Countess of Glencairn, with my lord and lady Betty, the Dean of Faculty, Sir John Whitefoord'.

Considering that the very first poem in his published collection was the conversation of the two dogs, in

James Cunningham, 14th Earl of Glencairn (1749–1791). Burns lamented his death with heartfelt grief and gratitude.
My noble master lies in clay;
The flower amang our barons bold,
His country's pride, his country's stay.
Engraving by D. O. Hill for Wilson and Chambers: The Land of Burns, *1840.*

'Caledonia's Bard, Brother Burns,' received into Canongate Kilwinning Lodge. From the painting by Stewart Watson.

which the habits of the aristocracy are described in such a scurrilous manner, their welcome to him appears all the more gracious. Yet they could not cure his pathological sense of social insecurity. In that same month of December he wrote to William Greenfield, another admirer, who was Professor of Rhetoric at the university and Minister of St Andrew's Church.

'Never did Saul's armour sit so heavy on David when going to encounter Goliath as does the encumbering robe of public notice with which the friendship and patronage of some "names dear to fame" have invested me. I do not say this in the ridiculous idea of seeming self-abasement, and affected modesty. I have long studied myself, and I think I know pretty exactly what ground I occupy, both as a Man and a Poet; and however the world, or a friend, may sometimes differ from me in that particular, I stand for it, in silent resolve, with all the tenaciousness of Property. I am willing to believe that my abilities deserved a better fate than the veriest shades of life; but to be dragged forth, with all my imperfections on my head, to the full glare of learned and polite observation, is what, I am afraid, I shall have bitter reason to repent.'

Why? The learned and polite observation of such men as Henry Erskine and Dugald Stewart had already fed his self-esteem to the extent that Mrs Allison Cockburn, author of *Flowers of the Forest*, observed, 'The man will be spoiled if he can spoil.' Burns certainly could not spoil, but he could and did add a tendency to back into the limelight to his other self-dramatizations. He continued his letter to Professor Greenfield: 'I mention this to you, once for all,

merely, in the confessor style, to disburden my conscience, and that – "When proud Fortune's ebbing tide recedes" [a quotation from Shenstone] – you may bear me witness, when my bubble of fame was at the highest, I stood, unintoxicated, with the inebriating cup in my hand, looking forward, with rueful resolve, to the hastening time when the stroke of envious Calumny, with all the eagerness of vengeful triumph, should dash it to the ground.'

There was to be no envious calumny or vengeful triumph. Burns had been received with an esteem never before accorded to a Scottish poet, in ducal drawing room and university precinct, masonic lodge and tavern. Only his own behaviour could have secured the fulfilment of his prophecy; and it did. His conversation was the wonder of all who heard him, his manners were adaptable to every sort of social occasion, yet there were times when he seems to have been deliberately courting disaster. At a dinner table once, he rounded on a Minister of the Gospel with the remark, 'Sir, I perceive that a man may be an excellent judge of poetry by square and rule, and after all be a damned blockhead.' As Maria Riddell, the most intelligent and not the least long-suffering of the women whose friendship he enjoyed, was to remark, 'for every ten jokes he got a hundred enemies'. Unfortunately not all of his insults could be excused as jokes. He took his revenge on Miss Alexander of Ballochmyle for her objection to his poem about her by saying of her brothers, 'When Fate swore that their purses should be full, Nature was equally positive that their heads should be empty.'

Burns cannot be blamed for the society he preferred, for the most part younger men who were his intellectual inferiors, but with whom he shared a taste for bawdy conversation and sexual adventures. On the other hand, he need not have hurt the feelings of the kindly old blind Dr Blacklock, who had done so much to pave the way to his success, by neglecting to inform him of his arrival in Edinburgh. Neither had he any right to quarrel with the Earl of Glencairn's attentions to an undistinguished nobleman, when he himself had consorted with the teen-age clerk and draper in Mauchline. His attitude, in fact, exposes the inverted snobbery from which he suffered all his life.

Dugald Stewart, who possessed such a talent for encouraging the young, was another whom Burns came near to snubbing, if he did not actually do so. Stewart had followed up his kindness to the bard at his country home with vigorous promotion of his poems and a warm welcome to his Edinburgh circle of friends. But Burns sought more congenial company, so that Stewart recalled with regret, 'afterwards we met but seldom'.

One of the highest honours accorded to Burns was bestowed on him at a gathering of the Grand Lodge of Scotland, when the Grand Master gave a toast to 'Caledonia and Caledonia's Bard, Brother Burns'. That occurred in January, and on 1 February he was

William Smellie (1740–95).
'His uncombed grizzly locks, wild staring, thatched
A head for thought profound and clear, unmatched;
Yet though his caustic wit was biting-rude,
His heart was warm, benevolent and good.'
From a painting by an unknown artist. Scottish National
Portrait Gallery, Edinburgh.

received into the Canongate Kilwinning Lodge. A different sort of society into which he was introduced was the club known as the Crochallan Fencibles. It had been founded by William Smellie, who had become the first editor of the *Encyclopaedia Britannica* in 1771. Soon after his induction, Burns composed this portrait of the man.

> Shrewd Willie Smellie to Crochallan came;
> The old cocked hat, the grey surtout the same;
> His bristling beard just rising in its might,
> 'Twas four long nights and days to shaving night;
> His uncombed grizzly locks, wild staring,
>   thatched
> A head for thought profound and clear,
>   unmatched;
> Yet though his caustic wit was biting-rude,
> His heart was warm, benevolent and good.
> *Lines on William Smellie, 1787.*

In those last two lines, Burns might have been describing himself. One of his deepest personal misfortunes was that while he could be biting-rude to others, he was extremely vulnerable to any comparable slight to himself.

His inclination for the society of younger men who shared his less intellectual tastes led him, soon after his arrival in Edinburgh, into acquaintance with a convivial, womanizing law student named Robert Ainslie.

Above: The Two Bridges of Ayr *by Henry Duguid. Nineteenth-century pen and wash drawing. The subject of a spirited poem which Burns composed in 1786, relating a quarrel between the Auld Brig and the New Brig.*

Left: The memorial to the Gaelic bard Rob Donn Mackay (1714–1778) in the cemetery of Balnakil, Sutherland. The most similar poet to Robert Burns in Scottish literature, there seems to have been a resemblance even in their appearance. There is no surviving portrait of Rob Donn, but he was described as 'Brown-haired, brown-eyed, pale-complexioned, clear-skinned and I would say good-looking. When he entered a room his eye caught the whole at a glance, and the expression of his countenance always indicated much animation and energy. In figure he was rather below middle size, stout and well-formed according to his size.'

Opposite right: Mossgiel, where Burns first achieved the status, so dear to his family, of a tenant farmer, able to describe himself in his poetry as 'Rob Mossgiel'. Engraving by G. Cook from a drawing by J. O. Brown. Reproduced by courtesy of Mr Sam Gow.

Evening in a Scots Cottage, by Alexander Carse. Robert Burns's rather sentimental picture of peasant life in 'The Cotter's Saturday Night', dedicated to Robert Aiken the Lawyer, found great favour with Mrs Dunlop of Dunlop, and other members of polite society.

Robert Ainslie (1766–1838), the womanizing law student with whom Burns toured the Border country, a pillar of respectablity in later life. From the engraving by J. Cochran.

Like Richard Brown the sailor of Irvine and John Richmond the clerk from Mauchline, Ainslie later became a pillar of respectability and vied with the others in dissociating himself from some of the tales of his earlier association with the bard. But Ainslie was certainly the friend to whom Burns turned when a casual affair with a servant called May Cameron led (as usual) to her pregnancy. 'Send for the wench and give her ten or twelve shillings, but don't for Heaven's sake meddle with her as a Piece,' he told Ainslie, and asked him to try to persuade her to return to the country. 'You may not like the business, but I must tax your friendship this far.'

Others may not have liked the business any better, but it is doubtful whether Burns suffered much prejudice on account of it. Such peccadillos were too much the order of the day. Nor could his presence at the tavern gatherings of the Crochallan Fencibles, for whom he composed so many of his best bawdy poems, have raised many eyebrows. People of all classes frequented the tavern clubs. Not even his preference for the company of Robert Ainslie to that of Dugald Stewart or his professed prejudice against what he called 'the noblesse' can be held accountable for his social failure in Edinburgh. He showed in practice a great deal more attention to the Earl of Glencairn than to the old poet Dr Blacklock, who was a humble

bricklayer's son. He fell because he, who studied his own feelings so assiduously, was careless of the feelings of others.

Mrs Dunlop discovered this, as Jean Armour and May Cameron did. This admittedly rather tiresome woman had been among the first to flatter him with her praise. She had also distributed his book in influential circles. One copy she sent to Dr Moore, father of the General who died at Corunna, who interested the Earl of Eglinton in his turn. Mrs Dunlop also took the practical step of looking for a sinecure that might provide Burns with a secure income. 'When your book reached Edinburgh,' she wrote to him in March 1787, 'Mr Smith, Commissioner of the Customs, suggested a thing which might be procured, and which he said was just what he would have wished for himself had he been in narrow circumstances – being a Salt officer. Their income is from £30 to £40, their duty easy, independent, and free from that odium or oppression attached to the Excise.'

Adam Smith had already reached his peak of European celebrity with *The Wealth of Nations*. He was seriously ill when Burns reached Edinburgh, and went to London after his recovery, which prevented him from assisting the bard. At a time when a school teacher's salary averaged £20, the one he proposed for Robert Burns was far from contemptible. Mrs Dunlop suggested next a career in the army, which Burns considered sympathetically before rejecting it. Finally, after all the months of delay, he agreed to give his motherly fan the treat she had craved for so long. He accepted her invitation to visit Dunlop House and there meet her for the first time.

He knew her to be a lonely widow, disappointed in her son. Her letters told Burns of her expectation and the care with which she had prepared for his entertainment faced him on his arrival. Yet he behaved with such boorishness that Mrs Dunlop was incensed into repaying him in his own coin. She composed satirical verses on the occasion which reveal her as a lady of spirit and wit. Some of the comments on the bard are placed in the mouths of her servants.

> Giff that be Burns, he may [hae lear]
> [have learning]
> But faith! I'm sure he has nae mair.
> He's brought his [havins] frae the [manners]
> plough,
> Ne'er touched his hat nor made a bow;
> Lap on his horse an' pu'd his coat thegither,
> Clashed to the Major's gin he'd been his brither.
> He may write books but by his [gate]
> [behaviour]
> He's little sense and verra great conceit.

Fortunately the episode did not terminate their friendship. It was not until near the end of his life that Burns did or said something which reduced the warm, voluble Mrs Dunlop to an icy silence.

An interesting aspect of her poem is that it reflects

Above: Burns in the home of James Burnett, Lord Monboddo (1714–1799), in St John Street, Edinburgh. A native of Kincardineshire like the father of Burns, Monboddo anticipated the Darwinian theory of the origin of species. From the painting by James Edgar in the Scottish National Portrait Gallery, Edinburgh.

Below: Burns in the home of Dr Adam Ferguson (1723–1816) in The Sheens, Edinburgh. A Professor of Natural Philosophy, Ferguson derived from Perthshire and possessed a knowledge of Gaelic from which Burns might have benefited if he had been so inclined. This painting by C. M. Hardie celebrates his sole meeting with Walter Scott, then a boy of fifteen, when Dugald Stewart was also present.

Above: The Black Stool, *by David Allan, 1784. The Calvinist Sabbath was enlivened by the appearance of sinners on the stool of penitence at public worship, whose offences were expounded by the Minister. Burns was grateful to the Rev. Dr Auld for permitting him merely to stand in his place while he was reprimanded for committing fornication with Jean Armour.*

Opposite left: Burns and Highland Mary at Failford, *by W. H. Midwood. The most romanticized of the bard's sexual adventures. Reproduced by courtesy of the Trustees of Burns Cottage and Monument, Alloway.*

Right: Jean Armour (1767–1834) in later life. Watercolour by Samuel Mackenzie, c. 1820.

P O E M S,

CHIEFLY IN THE

SCOTTISH DIALECT.

BY
R O B E R T   B U R N S.

EDINBURGH,
PRINTED FOR THE AUTHOR,
AND SOLD BY WILLIAM CREECH.
M,DCC,LXXXVII.

the enthusiasm of aristocratic ladies for the country vernacular. Dr Blacklock, the bricklayer's son from Annan, by contrast was among the many who had no use for it, composing instead in the modern English which had been the language of letters in Scotland for a century and more. Paradoxically, it was not such as he who advocated the preservation of the old tongue for the most part, but a section of genteel society. Perhaps if England had been governed from Edinburgh, rather than Scotland from London, there might have been a literary movement in the southern metropolis promoting a return to the language of Chaucer, enriched by the old dialects of the countryside.

It is perfectly obvious that William Burness had reared his family with the views of a Dr Blacklock. The Bible that was his principal reading was in stately standard English, and this must have been the language of his family, even if his inflections came from eastern Scotland while his wife's belonged to Ayrshire. Dugald Stewart could not have described the speech of Robert Burns as he did if this had not been so. 'Nothing was more remarkable among his various attainments, than the fluency, and precision, and originality of his language, when he spoke in company, more particularly as he aimed at purity in his turn of expression, and avoided more successfully than most Scotchmen, the peculiarities of Scottish phraseology.'

Although the bard's letters are for the most part literary productions, carefully composed, they are lit by many flashes which seem to illuminate him as he held a company spellbound by the magic of his conversation. On the other hand his brother Gilbert's letters, which are fluent, unlaboured and unadorned, preserve more faithfully the voices of the fireside at which he and Robert were reared. It was here that the vernacular poetry of Robert Fergusson fell on Burns like a thunderbolt, marking him deeply with its influence. When he reached Edinburgh, he erected a headstone over Fergusson's grave, one of the most symbolic gestures of his life.

But his immediate purpose in visiting the capital, as he had told Mrs Dunlop before he set out, was to publish a second edition of his poems there. Help and encouragement poured in from all sides. Glencairn introduced him to William Creech, the city's leading publisher and formerly the Earl's tutor. 'I am nearly agreed with Creech to print my book,' he told John Ballantine as early as 13 December 1786, and towards the end of the following March had finished correcting the proofs. Glencairn, two Dukes and other members of the noblesse were so assiduous in raising subscriptions that the edition was exhausted before it appeared, so that the text had to be hastily reset to print a third.

In them Burns released some of the gems he had withheld from the Kilmarnock edition on various grounds. For instance there was his playful satire called *Death and Dr Hornbook*, too easily identified as the schoolmaster of Tarbolton who augmented his salary by giving medical advice and dispensing drugs. Burns represented Death as castigating the quack for

Above right: The High Street, Edinburgh, *by Henry Duguid. A 19th-century impression.*

Right: Burns in Edinburgh, *by C. M. Hardie. Left to right: Henry Erskine, Dugald Stewart, the Dowager Countess of Glencairn, Adam Ferguson, Robert Burns, Hugh Blair, William Tytler, Henry Mackenzie, William Creech, Alexander Naysmith, Lord Monboddo, the Earl of Glencairn, Margaret Chalmers, Jane, Duchess of Gordon, Miss Burnett, Thomas Blacklock and William Marshall the butler. Reproduced by courtesy of Irvine Burns Club.*

Left: Baxter's Close, Edinburgh, *by Henry Duguid, where Burns shared the lodgings of John Richmond on his arrival in the capital in 1786.*

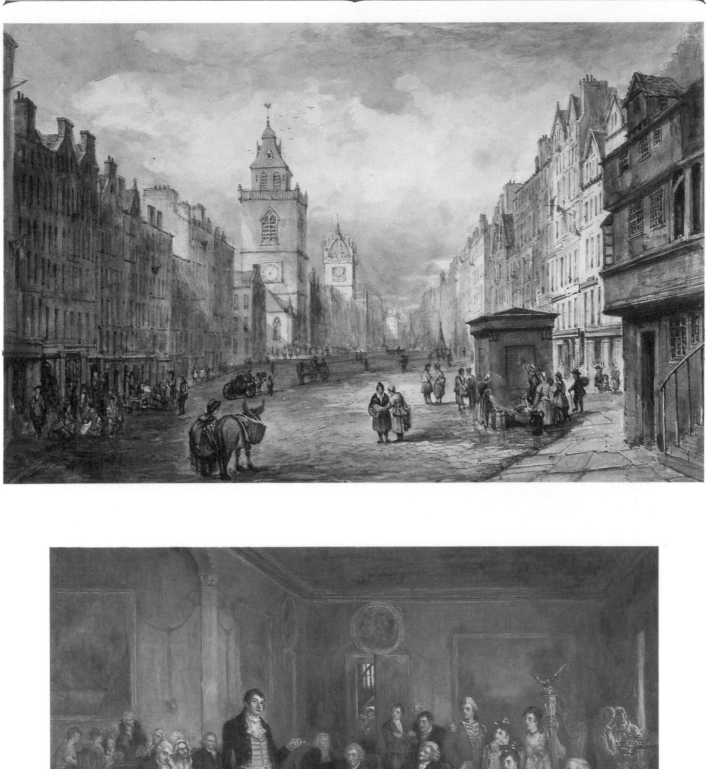

usurping his functions and depriving him of his occupation. Another notable addition to the new volume was the *Address to the Unco Guid, or the Rigidly Righteous*, an attack on intolerance with its plea for compassion.

> Then gently scan your brother Man,
> Still gentler sister Woman;
> Though they may gang a [kennin]   [little]
>   wrang,
> To step aside is human:
> One point must still be greatly dark,
> The moving *Why* they do it;
> And just as lamely can ye mark,
> How far perhaps they rue it.

There had been surprisingly few songs in the earlier edition. Of the seven he now added, by far the most interesting is *Green Grow the Rashes O*, not only for its intrinsic beauty but because it is an early sample of Burns' gift for reworking fragments of folk-verse and marrying them to traditional airs. Here he has improved upon earlier, bawdy versions, as bowdlerizers so often fail to do, and set them to a dance tune which had been written in an incipient form early in the 17th century. It was a portent of his final literary achievement.

As for the choice he made in adding twenty-two poems to his former collection, he told Mrs Dunlop during the month in which he was correcting his proofs, 'I have the advice of some very judicious friends among the Literati here, but with them I sometimes find it necessary to claim the privilege of thinking for myself.' Not always, unfortunately. Dr Hugh Blair, who had helped to foist the bogus Ossian epics on the bard and so many others besides, evidently dissuaded him from including that marvellously authentic celebration of low life, the cantata of *The Jolly Beggars*. It was not published until after his death, and its very survival in manuscript is something of a wonder.

Another notable omission is *Holy Willie's Prayer*, perhaps the most consummate satire ever composed in the English language: and it *is* composed in the English language, with only minimal concessions to local pronunciation. The subject of it was an identifiable Elder of the Church, and it is a withering attack on the doctrine of Election upheld by Calvinist fundamentalists. This suffices to account for its suppression until it appeared anonymously in a pamphlet of 1789.

Of all the newly-printed poems the most familiar throughout the world is the address *To a Haggis*, a dish of the poor that consists in the offal of the sheep, cooked in its stomach with oatmeal and onions. Today, thanks to Burns, it has become fashionable, and his poem is recited at every Burns Night supper that commemorates his birthday, when it is brought to the table.

The Jolly Beggars. *Pen and Wash drawing by Alexander Carse.*
Does the train-attended CARRIAGE
Thro' the country lighter rove?
Does the sober bed of MARRIAGE
Witness brighter scenes of love?

In addition to the subscriptions for his book, the bard received a fee for the copyright from William Creech of a hundred guineas. This amount was negotiated by Henry Mackenzie, whose novel *The Man of Feeling* Burns admired so greatly, and although it appears paltry today, no such sum had been paid for a collection of poems in Scotland in living memory. It has been estimated that in the end the bard received about £850 from the copyright fee and subscriptions, after he had paid the cost of printing, which he had to bear himself. Doubtless he might have earned far more if he had enjoyed the services of a competent literary agent of the modern sort, but by the standards of the day what he received was far from negligible.

Unfortunately Creech was dilatory in paying, which led to considerable acrimony until he met his obligations in March 1789. Burns then displayed the generosity of character that was never far beneath the surface of his somewhat irascible nature. 'I was at Edinburgh lately, and finally settled with Mr Creech; and I must retract some ill-natured surmises in my last letter, and own that at last, he has been amicable and fair with me.' It was more than Creech deserved.

In the case of the Earl of Glencairn it was the other way round. That nobleman little deserved Robert's criticism of the society he kept, but fully merited the bard's final tribute.

> The bridegroom may forget the bride,
> Was made his wedded wife yestreen;
> The monarch may forget the crown
> That on his head an hour has been;
> The mother may forget the child
> That smiles sae sweetly on her knee;
> But I'll remember thee, Glencairn,
> And a' that thou hast done for me!
>
> *Lament for James, Earl of Glencairn.*

The Kilmarnock edition had transformed Burns into Caledonia's Bard: the Edinburgh one advanced him rapidly to the rank of one of the world's poets. It was issued simultaneously in London and soon afterwards in America. There were the snide and silly criticisms, such as all authors must learn to expect, but it does not suffice to explain the bard's state of mind as he reflected on his fresh triumph. This followed its predictable course, and the unwary Mrs Dunlop was among those who bore the brunt of it. 'Your criticisms, Madam, I understand very well, and could have wished to have pleased you better. You are right in your guesses that I am not very amenable to counsel. Poets, much my superiors, have so flattered those who possessed the adventitious qualities of wealth and power that I am determined to flatter no created being, either in prose or verse, so help me God. I set as little by kings, lords, clergy, critics, etc. as all these respectable Gentry do by my Bardship. I know what I may expect from the world, by and by; illiberal abuse and perhaps

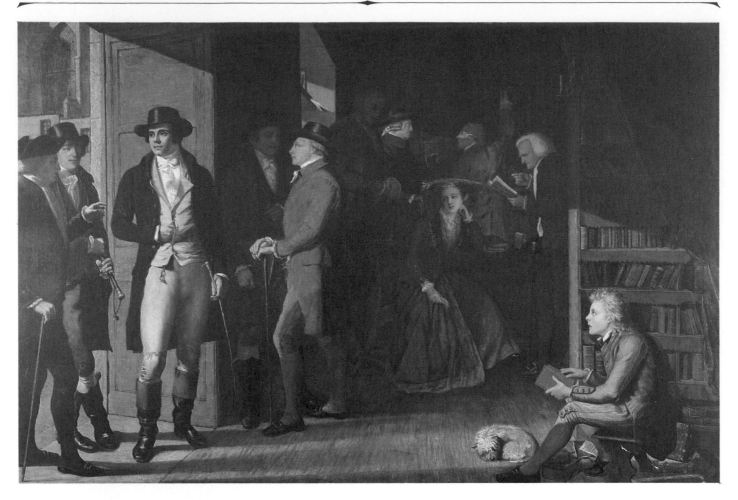

Burns at Sibbald's Library, *by William Borthwick Johnson. Left to right: Hugh Blair, Henry Mackenzie, Robert Burns, Alexander Naysmith, David Allan, James Bruce of Kinnaird, Lord Monboddo, Miss Burnett, Mr Sibbald, Adam Ferguson and the young Walter Scott. Lady Stair's House, Edinburgh.*

Below: Smellie's Printing Office in Anchor Close, Edinburgh, *by Henry Duguid. William Smellie, who founded the* Encyclopaedia Britannica *long before Burns came to Edinburgh, was among his companions in the tavern club there known as The Crochallan Fencibles.*

Margaret Chalmers (1763?–1843), daughter of a gentleman
farmer of Ayrshire, the one acquaintance with whom Burns
might have enjoyed a marriage of true minds as well as bodies.
From an oil painting by John Irvine, c. 1800, in the possession
of W. F. Watson, Edinburgh.

Melrose Abbey, which Burns visited during his tour of the Border country with Robert Ainslie in May 1787. He told Ainslie in July: 'I have not a friend upon earth, besides yourself, to whom I can talk nonsense without forfeiting some degree of his esteem.'

contemptuous neglect: but I am resolved to study the sentiments of a very respectable Personage, Milton's Satan – "Hail horrors! hail, Infernal world!"'

So far from living up to the determination he expressed to Mrs Dunlop, Burns composed some dreadfully turgid verses on the Lord President, Robert Dundas, when he died in 1787 and sent them 'with my best prose letter, to the Son of the Great Man the theme of the Piece, by the hands too of one of the noblest men in God's world'. Robert was the half-brother of Henry Dundas, later Lord Melville, who ran Scotland like one huge rotten borough until he became the last politician in Britain to suffer impeachment for corruption. Perhaps the Dundas family had read the lampoon on the behaviour of their class in the poem of the two dogs, or had heard one of the Bard's jibes about the Noblesse. At any rate, they 'took no more notice of my Poem or me than I had been a strolling Fiddler who had made free with his lady's name over the head of a

silly new reel! Did the gentleman think I looked for any dirty gratuity?' Very probably; and the poem hardly deserved it.

A man who sent Burns a most handsome gratuity of ten guineas, anonymously, was Patrick Miller, brother of the Lord Justice Clerk, an Ayrshire laird. Miller was chairman of the Carron Company, which had been established a couple of decades earlier to exploit coal for the smelting of iron, when it was the largest planned undertaking of its kind in Europe and marked the beginning of heavy industry in Scotland. A versatile entrepreneur, Miller had recently bought a neglected estate at Dalswinton in Dumfriesshire, and he conceived a notion that the farmer–poet might be the right man to improve it. Burns responded cautiously. 'Mr Miller is no Judge of land,' he remarked to his friend John Ballantine the banker, 'and though I dare say he means to favour me, yet he may give me, in his opinion, an advantageous bargain that may ruin me.'

Miller himself was to write, 'When I went to view my purchase, I was so much disgusted for eight or ten days that I meant never to return to this country.' But he thought the 170 acres of Ellisland, although in a 'most miserable state of exhaustion', as he found them, might be improved. Instead of making a careful inspection of the property in the light of Miller's generous terms, followed by a definite decision, Burns vacillated for over a year in his characteristic way before committing himself. Neither did he exploit the other opportunities that were open to him to find a secure form of livelihood while he was surrounded by well-wishers in Edinburgh. On 5 May, with his book launched and money in his pocket, he set out on the first of a series of jaunts throughout the country.

The companion of his tour through the Border country was the law student Robert Ainslie, and the journal he kept during their travels reveals that Burns looked on nature with the eye of a most average-minded sightseer. It was not here that his inspiration lay. On the other hand he sent to William Nicol, a brother freemason in Edinburgh who was a Latin teacher, the only letter he ever composed in the Scottish vernacular. It may seem surprising that he never wrote thus to his Ayrshire friends, but these received instead his marvellous, racy epistles in verse. He had already published some of these in the Kilmarnock edition, those to the son of Robert Aiken the lawyer, and to David Siller and James Smith of the Tarbolton Bachelors' Club.

He examined the Ellisland property, still without making up his mind, then returned to Mossgiel early in June after his six months' absence. He had already subsidized his family generously out of his subscription money and now he was in their midst again, a national celebrity. According to his own harsh comment, the Armours received him with servile compliance. Jean did no less, so that in due course Burns informed Mrs Dunlop: 'the usual consequences began to betray her'. But he remained disorientated, uncertain about his future; and his muse appears to have deserted him.

He turned his steps towards the most accessible region of the Highlands, the mountains of Argyll, and this time he neither took a companion nor kept a journal. Romantic speculation has supposed that he was visiting the Campbell country to visit the grave of his lost love and savour the society in which she had been reared. There is not the slightest evidence that this was his motive. As for the reactions of the author of *My Heart's in the Highlands*, he told Robert Ainslie on 25 June: 'I write this on my tour through a country where savage streams tumble over savage mountains, thinly spread with savage flocks, which starvingly support as savage inhabitants.' Such was his reaction to the surroundings which Duncan Macintyre was still celebrating in his hymns to nature. If Burns heard any of these, or the products of the other greatest Scottish song composers of his time, Rob Donn and Alexander MacDonald, he never said so.

He returned to Edinburgh in August, presumably in an attempt to extract money from William Creech, which proved counter-productive when May Cameron, not content with her ten or twelve shillings, issued a writ against her seducer. By the end of the month William Nicol was free to accompany him on

Coldstream, whose bridge crosses the Tweed not far from the site of the fatal battle of Flodden, fought in 1513. Here Burns first stepped on English soil on 7 May 1787. From Allan Cunningham: Pictures and Portraits of the Life and Land of Robert Burns, 1840.

Newcastle, the most southerly town that Burns visited during his Border tour. Drawn by W. Westall, engraved by F. Francis for Great Britain Illustrated, 1830.

Eyemouth, where both Burns and Ainslie were made Royal Arch Masons of the Local lodge. Burns's membership was honorary but Ainslie had to pay a guinea. From Skene's Sketches, 1829.

Stirling Castle. From Francis Grose: The Antiquities of Scotland, *1797.*

Gordon Castle, today a ruin, which Burns visited in the company of William Nicol. Engraving by D. O. Hill for Wilson and Chambers: The Land of Burns, *1840.*

the third of his tours, which they made in a small carriage. It took them by way of Bannockburn, which Burns was to celebrate some six years later in his song *Scots, wha hae wi' Wallace bled*, (Robert Bruce's March to Bannockburn) and to Stirling, where he used a diamond ring that Glencairn had given him to scratch Jacobite lines on a tavern window-pane. They compare extremely unfavourably with the Jacobite songs of Alexander MacDonald.

> The injur'd Stewart-line are gone,
> A Race outlandish fill their throne;
> An idiot race, to honour lost;
> Who know them best despise them most.
>
> *Lines on Stirling.*

The lines appear equally crude by comparison with Rob Donn's indictment of the house of Hanover.

It was otherwise when Burns was led by affection, rather than irrational prejudice, in the paths where his true genius lay. On his journey north through Perthshire, eastwards from Inverness by way of Moray, and then down the broad peninsula that faces the North Sea in which his Burness ancestors had lived, he listened to folk-songs in a language he could understand and his imagination caught fire. His lyric gift returned to him as he snatched at scraps of verse and memorized the tunes he heard. This was the area in which his taste was to prove infallible, his inventiveness most rich. Countless songs and airs might have been lost if he had not rescued them, or would not have survived in the beautiful form in which he presented them.

He permitted himself to be dined by the Duke and Duchess of Atholl at Blair castle, and this was fortunate, because Graham of Fintry was among the guests, a Commissioner of the Excise. The Duke and Duchess of Gordon invited him to stay at Gordon castle as he made his way south into Aberdeenshire; but William Nicol took offence when he was not greeted with equal attention and persuaded the bard to leave prematurely. He passed through Stonehaven where he could survey the ruins of Dunnottar castle, in which his grandfather had worked as gardener before its destruction in the aftermath of the 1715 uprising. Here too, he met his cousin the lawyer, whom he found to be 'one of these who love fun, a gill, a punning joke, and have not a bad heart – his wife a sweet hospitable body, without any affectation of what is called town-breeding'. Farther south in Montrose 'I spent two days among our relations, and found our aunts, Jean and Isabel still alive and hale old women.' So he returned with Nicol to Edinburgh, determined that this time he would induce Creech to settle with him, but still undecided whether to accept the offer of Ellisland.

Instead he went off on a fourth tour, this time in the company of Dr James Adair, a friend of the Minister of Loudoun who had first introduced his poetry to Dr Blacklock in Edinburgh. This latest escapade is chiefly memorable for his association with Margaret Chalmers, a distant relative of Gavin Hamilton, who used to read and sing to the blind Dr Blacklock. He spent eight days in her company at Harvieston house.

Here at last was a girl with whom he might have enjoyed a lifelong meeting of minds as well as bodies, the daughter of a gentleman farmer of Ayrshire who could share his intellectual interests. He addressed her more than once as though he had desired nothing more. 'When you whisper, or look kindly to another, it gives me a draught of damnation,' he once told her, and surely such a man as Robert Burns might have won her if he had really tried. Months after their parting he could still write: 'When I think I have met with you, and have lived more of real life with you in eight days than I can do with almost anybody I meet with in eight years – when I think on the improbability of meeting you in this world again – I could sit down and cry like a child!'

What he actually did, little over a month after he had parted from Margaret Chalmers, was to sit down and write to another woman, with whom he was barely acquainted: 'I can say with truth, Madam, that I never met with a person in my life whom I more anxiously wished to meet again than yourself.' Burns had not changed since the days when he made mutually exclusive protestations to Mary Campbell and Jean Armour, though now he was addressing them to girls not so accessible to what he called his 'dearest member'.

Agnes M'Lehose was a married woman of about the same age as Burns whose husband had separated from her and lived in Jamaica, leaving her penniless. She seems to have become infatuated even before she engineered her first meeting with the bard on 6 December, after his return to Edinburgh, and in the tragi-

John Murry, 4th Duke of Atholl (1755–1830). As a guest at Blair Atholl on 31 August 1787, Burns first made the acquaintance of Robert Graham of Fintry, who was to prove a good friend in the future. From the portrait by John Hoppner in the collection of the Duke of Atholl at Blair Castle.

comedy that ensued he used every weapon in his armoury in an attempt to seduce her. But she depended on her uncle Lord Craig, a Court of Session judge, for her maintenance, while her morals were guarded by the formidable Minister of the Tolbooth Church, the Rev. John Kemp. As he sought a passage between Scylla and Charybdis, she alternately beckoned him on and warned him back, in prose and verse.

> Your Friendship much can make me blest,
> O, why that bliss destroy!
> Why urge the odious, one request
> You know I must deny!

The sparring match continued throughout the winter, in private meetings that did not quite overstep the 'limits of Virtue', and in letters in which they addressed one another as Clarinda and Sylvander. Burns consoled himself for the refusal of his odious request in the arms of a servant named Jenny Clow, who became pregnant like the others.

But after the rather aimless and indecisive months of wandering, Burns found at last a new outlet for his enthusiasm and talents during this second winter in Edinburgh, so that he did not merely dissipate his energies in flirtation. On 25 October he wrote to John Skinner, author of a song called *O Tullochgorum's my*

Robert Burns. The silhouette by John Miers. Scottish National Portrait Gallery, Edinburgh.

delight, set to what was originally an instrumental tune. This was an art that Burns was to bring to perfection, and now the opportunity had been laid before him. 'There is a work going on in Edinburgh, just now, which claims your best assistance. An engraver in this town has set about collecting and publishing all the Scotch songs, with the music, that can be found.' James Johnson's *Scots Musical Museum* was to be the first systematically documented collection of its kind to appear in print, and to it Burns devoted himself for the remainder of his life, refusing any fee for his work. It was to be his gift to Scotland, and he did not even claim authorship when it was his due.

And now he took more positive steps to obtain a salaried job that would give him financial security. He wrote both to the ever-faithful Earl of Glencairn and to Robert Graham of Fintry, to whom he had been introduced in ducal company at Blair Atholl, asking them to help him obtain a post as Officer of Excise. Then he turned his face westwards towards the end of February, called to see Jean Armour where she was staying in the home of his friend William Muir at Tarbolton, and so arrived home again at Mossgiel.

Immediately he wrote to Clarinda, and described his meeting with Jean. 'I am disgusted with her; I cannot endure her! I, while my heart smote me for the profanity, tried to compare her with my Clarinda; 'twas setting the expiring glimmer of a farthing taper beside the cloudless glory of the meridian sun. Here was

tasteless insipidity, vulgarity of soul, and mercenary fawning; there, polished good sense, heaven-born genius, and the most generous, the most delicate, the most tender Passion. I have done with her, and she with me.' As the world knows, they had done no such thing.

Sylvander also told Clarinda, as soon as he had arrived at Mossgiel, of his intention to revisit the farm of Ellisland. 'I set off tomorrow for Dumfriesshire. 'Tis merely out of compliment to Mr Miller, for I know the Excise must be my lot.' Alas, this proved to be a false prediction also. Burns took with him an older man on whose advice he felt that he could rely, John Tennant of Glenconner, who regarded Patrick Miller's terms as a bargain. Robert signed a lease on 13 March, then returned to Edinburgh, where he was accepted as a candidate for the Excise on the 31st and sent to Tarbolton for a three weeks' course of training. And during that month he sealed his future fate in a still more decisive way.

Despite what he had said a few days earlier about the farthing taper, and although Jean Armour was within a few weeks of her confinement, Burns wrote of her to Robert Ainslie on 3 March: 'I have taken her to my arms: I have given her a mahogany bed: I have given her a guinea; and I have f——d her till she rejoiced with joy unspeakable and full of glory. But – as I always am on every occasion – I have been prudent and cautious to an astounding degree; I swore her, privately and solemnly, never to attempt any claim on me as a husband, even though anybody should persuade her she had such a claim, which she has not, neither during my life, nor after my death. She did all this like a good girl, and I took the opportunity of some dry horselitter, and gave her such a thundering scalade that electrified the very marrow of her bones.' He wrote those words on the day Jean was once again delivered of twins, and it is hardly surprising that neither of these survived.

By the end of April the bard was writing to his friend James Smith the linen draper, 'to let you into the secrets of my pericranium, there is, you must know, a certain clean-limbed, handsome, bewitching young hussy of your acquaintance, to whom I have lately and privately given a matrimonial title to my corpus'. Gradually he leaked the same information to his family, to the editor of the *Scots Musical Museum*, to Robert Ainslie who must have been as surprised as any. But he did not tell Clarinda, leaving her to find out by hearsay.

She relapsed into a year's shocked silence before writing him a letter which is lost, so that its contents can only be guessed from his sanctimonious, self-righteous reply. 'When you call over the scenes that have passed between us, you will survey the conduct of an honest man, struggling successfully with temptations the most powerful that ever beset humanity, and preserving untainted honour in situations where the austerest Virtue would have forgiven a fall – Situations that I will dare to say, not a single individual of all his kind, even with half his sensibility and passion, could have encountered without ruin . . .' Of all the bard's self-dramatizations, this picture of a man of unassailable morals, repelling the almost irresistible temptations of a harpy, like Odysseus tied to the mast, is among the most hilarious.

But why did Burns so suddenly marry Jean Armour, after all the scurrilous remarks he had made about her to all and sundry? He had recently completed his training for the Excise, whose Commissioners may well have been concerned about the irregularity of his personal life. It has been suggested that they might have insisted on his marriage as a condition of his employment, and although there is no evidence for this, no more plausible explanation has been found for the step he took.

On 5 August 1788 the union was recorded formally by the Church Session of Mauchline, and five days later Burns offered to Mrs Dunlop this specious explanation for his failure to choose a more appropriate spouse. 'Circumstanced as I am, I could never have got a female Partner for life who could have entered into my favourite studies, relished my favourite Authors, &c, without entailing on me, at the same time, expensive living, fantastic caprice, apish affectation, with all the other blessed Boarding-school acquirements.' It is a misogynist's view of the opposite sex, penned by a man to whom women were a necessity in the byre and the bed.

By the time he wrote those words, Robert was installed in Ellisland, and he had received his commission as an officer of the Excise 'reposing especial Trust, and confidence in the Knowledge, Skill, Industry,

Robert Burns. A chalk drawing by Alexander Skirving, who never set eyes on the poet. Scottish National Portrait Gallery, Edinburgh.

Integrity, Fidelity and Circumspection of Robert Burns Gentleman'.

'Burns and Jean Armour began house keeping in 1788.' Drawing by James Torrence of the house in Mauchline in which they lived between their marriage and the move to Ellisland.

Chapter 5

FROM JUNE 1788 until May 1789 Burns battled with the builders who were erecting his new home at Ellisland. Patrick Miller had advanced £300 to pay for the dwelling house and the enclosure of fields. Robert lived meanwhile in the hut that had sufficed the previous farmer, while Jean remained at Mossgiel, some forty-five miles away, learning the secrets of dairy management from the bard's mother. These were inauspicious circumstances in which to try to create a prosperous farm out of neglected land. Burns wrote to his mason on 8 February, in the depths of his first winter there: 'I am distressed with the want of my house in a most provoking manner. It loses me two hours' work of my servants every day, besides other inconveniences. For God's sake let me but within the shell of it!'

Not least of the inconveniences was the distance that separated him from his wife, which moved him to compose one of his most tender love songs, set to the air of a strathspey.

> There's wild-woods grow, and rivers [row],   [roll]
> And money a hill between;
> But day and night my fancy's flight
> Is ever wi' my Jean.
>
> I love my Jean, to the tune,
Miss Admiral Gordon's Strathspey.

In 1788, he also delivered the most famous song in the world on the subject of reunion and separation, with its opening challenge: 'Should auld acquaintance be forgot and never brought to mind?' During the three and a half busy years the bard was to spend at Ellisland he did not produce much poetry, but it includes some of his best.

His difficulties were compounded by the responsibilities he bore as a conscientious head of the family. He had lost one of the twins born to Jean in 1786, but there were still Elizabeth Paton's daughter at Mossgiel, his little son Robert, his mother, his two brothers and three sisters. When Uncle Robert Burness died in January, his daughter and two sons were added to the household. The bard's younger brother William proved something of a problem, so that Burns took him in charge at Ellisland as soon as he was able, until finally William obtained work as a saddler in London.

Amongst the letters of fatherly advice the bard sent him was his response to the news that William was in love. 'I am, you know, a veteran in these campaigns, so let me advise you always to pay your particular assiduities and try for intimacy as soon as you feel the first symptoms of passion.' Inadequate as William appears

Robert Graham (1749–1815), the 12th laird of Fintry, the Commissioner of the Excise to whom Burns was introduced by the Duke of Atholl at Castle Blair. Silhouette in the possession of his family.

Dumfries in the early 19th century. From an engraving by J. Ramage.

to have been in many ways, he had evidently not enjoyed his brother's success as a lover before he died in London in July 1790.

Much depended on the first harvest at Ellisland, and it proved to be a poor one. When that of 1789 was equally unprofitable, Burns found himself unable to put more capital into his enterprise because he had placed £180 in the hands of Gilbert for the rescue of Mossgiel. His solution was to apply for the Excise post for which he was now qualified. On 10 September he wrote to Graham of Fintry.

'Your Honourable Board, sometime ago, gave me my Excise Commission; which I regard as my sheet anchor in life. My farm, now that I have tried it a little, though I think it will in time be a saving bargain, yet does by no means promise to be such a Pennyworth as I was taught to expect. It is in the last stage of worn-out poverty, and will take some time before it pay the rent.' This amounted to £50 for the first three years with a rise thereafter. A post in the Excise would relieve him of this burden entirely, and there was a most suitable one that he would be able to fill without even having to leave his home, provided its present incumbent could be removed. Burns did not scruple to use the influence he had acquired by means of the noblesse to secure this.

'There is one way,' he continued his appeal to Robert Graham, 'by which I might be enabled to extricate myself from this embarrassment, a scheme which I hope and am certain is in your power to effectuate. I

Gilbert Burns (1760–1827), a silhouette perhaps executed by Howie in 1816. Scottish National Portrait Gallery, Edinburgh.

live here, Sir, in the very centre of a county Excise-Division; the present Officer lately lived on a farm which he rented in my nearest neighbourhood; and as a gentleman, owing to some legacies, is quite opulent, a removal could do him no manner of injury; and on a month's warning, to give me a little time to look over my Instructions, I would not be afraid to enter on Business.' He enclosed a complimentary poem in his most sycophantic vein.

> Why shrinks my soul, half-blushing, half afraid,
> Backward, abashed, to ask thy friendly aid?
> I know my need, I know thy giving hand,
> I tax thy friendship at thy kind command.
>> *To Robt. Graham of Fintry Esqr.,*
>> *with a request for an Excise Division.*

The lines had been lying in his drawer since the previous year, as though prepared in advance for just such a contingency. A radical and a leveller, Burns seems to have had some compunction over levelling someone wealthier than himself for his personal advantage. A little later he referred to his victim, whose name was Leonard Smith, in another letter to Graham. 'I could not bear to injure a poor fellow by ousting him to make way for myself; to the wealthy son of good fortune like Smith, the injury is imaginary where the propriety of your rules admits.' Evidently Graham concurred. In a month to the day from the date of the bard's application to him, the name of Burns was enrolled in the list of Excise officers. In a few weeks he was writing to his friend Robert Ainslie in his most contentedly philosophical mood.

'I am tired with and disgusted at the language of complaint against the evils of life. Human existence in the most favourable situations does not abound with pleasures, and has its inconveniences and ills; capricious, foolish Man mistakes these inconveniences and ills as if they were the peculiar property of his own particular situation; and hence that eternal fickleness, that love of change which has ruined and daily does ruin, many a fine fellow as well as many a Blockhead; and is almost without exception a constant source of

Excise returns signed by 'Rob! Burns'. From Lady Stair's House, Edinburgh.

disappointment and misery. So far from being dissatisfied with my present lot, I earnestly pray the Great Disposer of events that it may never be worse, and I think I may lay my hand on my heart and say, "I shall be content."'

It was to become tragically worse. He had already been prostrated in September by an attack of his chronic disease, and although he seems to have made at least a partial recovery by the time he wrote to Ainslie in these optimistic terms at the beginning of November, the winter soon took its toll again. On 13 December 1789 he told Mrs Dunlop: 'For now near three weeks I have been so ill with a nervous headache, that I have been obliged to give up for a time my Excise-books, being scarce able to lift my head, much less to ride once a week over ten muir Parishes.' Early in the New Year he confessed to his brother Gilbert: 'My nerves are in a damnable State. I feel that horrid hypochondria pervading every action of both body and soul. This farm has undone my enjoyment of myself. It is a ruinous affair on all hands. But let it go to hell! I'll fight it out and be off with it.'

His predecessor Leonard Smith had combined farming with his Excise duties, doubtless employing servants as Burns did, and the bard might well have succeeded as well if he had enjoyed better health. But he lived in a damp, low-lying area by the banks of the river Nith, the worst climate for his condition, in which he had been ill-housed for many months while his home was being built. But fight he did, with a courage most wonderful, although he did not know his real enemy, nor that it was impossible to win.

By his second winter at Ellisland he had embarked on a new occupation which involved travelling some two hundred miles a week on horseback in all weathers. It was his responsibility to ensure payment of duty on a host of articles in addition to alcohol in its many forms; candles and coaches, paper and pepper, salt and starch. He received £50, exactly the amount of his farm rent, as his annual salary: but in addition he enjoyed handsome perquisites in the form of fines and prize money. There were opportunities for promotion also, that might bring him far greater wealth than he or his family had ever wrung from the land. As usual the summer brought an improvement in his health, which he celebrated by making love to Anne Park, a servant in the Globe Tavern at Dumfries. His simultaneous attentions to his wife enabled them to give birth within a few days of one another.

Perhaps, in retrospect, Burns regretted that he had not aimed straight at the Excise the moment he was introduced to Robert Graham by the Duke of Atholl in the summer of 1787, instead of dawdling his way back into farming, and delaying for over two years before taking up his present post. Yet paradoxically this final spell of a way of life to which he had been accustomed all his days, and his ancestors before him, appears to have brought him great happiness despite the depressing bouts of illness and the financial worries. This is reflected in his correspondence with old acquaintances and the enlargement of his social life among new ones. Evidently Mary Campbell was still on his conscience, for it was in 1789 that he recalled their brief, mysterious association in his most nostalgic vein.

> Still o'er these scenes my mem'ry wakes,
> And fondly broods with miser-care;
> Time but th'impression stronger makes,
> As streams their channels deeper wear:
> My Mary, dear, departed Shade!
> Where is thy place of blissful rest?
>
> *A Song*, to the tune, *Captn. Cook's death.*

He must have known perfectly well where she was buried, whether or not he visited her grave in Greenock. A far finer song that he composed during this same year is also addressed to Mary, though the experts insist that its subject is not Mary Campbell.

> Flow gently sweet Afton, among thy green braes,
> Flow gently, sweet river, the theme of my lays;
> My Mary's asleep by thy murmuring stream,
> Flow gently, sweet Afton, disturb not her dream.
>
> *Afton Water.*

Whoever this Mary was, there is no doubt of the identity of Anne Park of the Globe Tavern, celebrated in the song of 1790.

> Yestreen I had a pint o' wine,
> A place where body saw na;
> Yestreen lay on this breast o' mine
> The gowden locks of Anna.
>
> *Song*, to the tune, *Banks of Banna.*

Amongst his old acquaintances, he exchanged verse epistles with Dr Blacklock, generous and solicitous as ever to the bard who had soared so high above him.

> Dear Burns, thou brother of my heart,
> Both for thy virtues and thy art;
> If art it may be called in thee,
> Which Nature's bounty large and free,
> With pleasure on thy breast diffuses,
> And warms thy soul with all the Muses.

Burns responded in the vernacular with one of his jolliest accounts of himself in his new office of Gauger, beginning:

> Wow, but your letter made me vauntie!
> And are ye hale, and weel, and [cantie]?
>
> [cheerful]

But his most regular correspondent remained Mrs Dunlop, to whom he sent his thoughts on religion, his poetical plans, drafts of what he had composed. She remained his mother-confessor throughout the Ellisland period, the recipient of his most candid comments in all his varying moods.

Of his new acquaintances by far the most important was Robert, son of Walter Riddell of Glenriddell. He had attended university and held a Captain's commis-

sion in the army before he retired, to marry Elizabeth
Kennedy from Manchester. They settled at Friar's
Carse, a rambling complex of buildings with a square
tower and crow-step gabled wing. There was a
hermitage in the grounds to which Burns was given the
key, so that he enjoyed a retreat from the hurly-burly of
his home in which he could write in peace. Friar's
Carse was transformed during the present century into
a convalescent and holiday home for Post Office
employees. Burns was to commemorate his own
entertainment there in the time of the Riddells with the
tribute: 'At their fireside I have enjoyed more pleasant
evenings than at all the houses of fashionable people in
this country put together; and to their kindness and
hospitality I am indebted for many of the happiest
years of my life.'

Captain Riddell was interested in antiquities, as the
editors of Camden's *Britannia* were aware when they
invited him to contribute information about south-
west Scotland for the new edition they were preparing.
He was also fond of music, and made *A Collection of
Scotch, Galwegian and Border Tunes for the violin and
pianoforte* which was published in 1794, the year of his
sudden death. At Friar's Carse Burns could enjoy the
cultivated society and intellectual stimulus that Jean
Armour could not provide at home. Nor was this all.
Captain Riddell was generous in helping the bard to

gather in his first harvest at Ellisland in 1788.

For this admirable neighbour Burns wrote out the
two volumes known as the Glenriddell manuscripts,
now in the Scottish National Library, containing selec-
tions of his poems and letters. He also presented to
Riddell a copy of James Johnson's *Scots Musical
Museum* with notes in his own hand on the contents.

There was also merriment at Friar's Carse, such as
Burns had enjoyed with the Tarbolton Bachelors and
the Crochallan Fencibles in Edinburgh. His ballad of
the whistle commemorates the evening of 16 October
1789, about the time when Burns began his duties as an
Excise officer. The whistle in question was a little
ebony one that had been brought to Scotland by one of
the attendants of Anne of Denmark, when she arrived
as the Queen of James VI. It used to be laid on the table
during drinking contests, and became the property of
the last man still able to blow it. So it was a souvenir of
the Danish custom to which Shakespeare referred in
Hamlet, when the Prince observed that it was 'more
honoured in the breach than the observance'.

The whistle had become the property of the Riddell
family, and on this particular evening the contenders
in the drinking bout included Sir Robert Lowrie, the
Member of Parliament for Dumfriesshire, and Alexander Fergusson of Craigdarroch who carried off the
prize. According to the later testimony of a servant,

Burns made no serious attempt to compete. 'When the gentlemen were put to bed, Burns walked home without any assistance.' Quite apart from the fact that he was far too busy to be able to lie in bed of a morning, sleeping off a hangover, his heart condition warned him increasingly against the dangers of heavy drinking, and he was recovering from a serious relapse at this very time. Gone were the days when he was prepared to pay for a convivial evening with a slice of his constitution. He did so instead with his ballad on the history of the whistle, and the latest contest in which it had been won.

> Next uprose our Bard, like a prophet in drink:
> 'Craigdarroch, thou'lt soar when creation shall
>   sink!
> 'But if thou would flourish immortal in rhyme,
> 'Come – one bottle more – and have at the
>   sublime.'
>
> *The Whistle. A Ballad.*

The most fortunate new acquaintance the bard found at Friar's Carse was Francis Grose, fortunate above all for Scottish literature. Grose was an antiquarian of Swiss origin who completed his publication of the *Antiquities of England and Wales* in 1787. In the following year he arrived to prepare a similar work on Scotland, and encountered the bard in the company of the Riddells at the time of the second disastrous harvest at Ellisland. Burns warned his countrymen:

> Hear, Land o' Cakes and brither Scots,
> Frae Maidenkirk to Johny Groats!
> If there's a hole in a' your coats,
>   I [rede you tent it].
>
>   [advise you to attend to it]
> A [chield]'s amang you, taking notes,   [fellow]
>   And, faith, he'll prent it.
>
> *On the Late Captain Grose's*
> *Peregrinations thro' Scotland.*

The two men took an instant liking to one another, and Burns urged Grose to include a picture of the old church of Alloway in his forthcoming publication. His father was buried there. Among all the places associated with the bard, there is none more evocative, more haunting, than this. Grose agreed, provided Burns undertook to compose a poem to accompany his illustration, and a note in his *Antiquities of Scotland* describes the theme he chose. 'This church is also famous for being the place wherein the witches and warlocks used to hold infernal meetings, or sabbaths, and prepare their magical unctions; here too they used to amuse themselves with dancing to the pipes of the

The competition for the whistle, witnessed by Burns.
Three joyous good fellows with hearts clear of flaw;
Craigdarroch so famous for wit, worth, and law;
And trusty Glenriddel, so skilled in old coins;
And gallant Sir Robert, deep-read in old wines.
From Allan Cunningham: Pictures and Portraits of the Life and
Land of Robert Burns, *1840.*

Francis Grose (c.1730–1791), *who inspired Burns's masterpiece*
of comic narration, Tam o' Shanter. *From the drawing by*
Nathaniel Dance. Scottish National Portrait Gallery,
Edinburgh.

Above: Alloway Kirk. From Francis Grose:
The Antiquities of Scotland, *1797.*

Right: While we sit bousing at the
            [nappy],   [ale]
And getting fou and unco happy,
We think na on the lang Scots miles,
The mosses, waters, slaps and styles,
That lie between us and our hame,
Whare sits our sulky sullen dame.
                              Tam o'Shanter.
Pen and ink drawing by Walter Geikie.

muckle-horned Deel. Diverse stories of these horrid rites are still current: one of which my worthy friend Mr Burns has here favoured me with in verse.' Thus Francis Grose succeeded in stimulating the bard to compose his last and perhaps greatest large-scale poem, that masterpiece of comic narration *Tam o' Shanter*.

In it he deployed the entire range of language at his command, from standard English to Ayrshire vernacular, which must have presented problems to translators. On the other hand, those who read *Tam o' Shanter* translated into their own tongues can hardly share the preoccupation of some of its author's countrymen over the language he used. Dr David Daiches, for instance, commenting on a stanza composed for the most part in English, surmised that Burns intended to be 'deliberate, cold, and formal'. He went further in reading the bard's mind. 'The English in these lines is a deliberately "fancy" English, piling up simile after simile as though to draw attention to the literary quality of utterance.' He chose another term to define this use of language when he asked: 'What more effective device than to employ a deliberate neo-classic English poetic diction in these lines?'

This is almost precisely the opposite view to one expounded by the late Douglas Young, a classical scholar who translated plays by Aristophanes into Scots. 'There is a deep-seated Scotticism,' wrote Young of the same stanza, 'counter-weighing the superficial Anglicism of stray words and, of course, Anglicised orthography.' Here is the passage in question, describing the familiar predicament, when a man must return home at last, possibly to an angry wife, after a too long and convivial night out. Not everyone will wish to spoil his enjoyment of it by pondering whether it is composed in 'Anglicised orthography' or in 'a deliberate neo-classic English poetic diction.' Fewer still will be able to decide whether Dr Daiches or Dr Young has read the intentions of Burns correctly.

> But pleasures are like poppies spread,
> You seize the flower, its bloom is shed;
> Or like the snow falls in the river,
> A moment white – then melts for ever;
> Or like the borealis race,
> That flits ere you can point their place;
> Or like the rainbow's lovely form
> Evanishing amid the storm.
> Nae man can tether time or tide;
> The hour approaches Tam maun ride;
> That hour, o' night's black arch the key-stane,
> That dreary hour he mounts his beast in;
> And sic a night he taks the road in,
> As ne'er poor sinner was abroad in.

It is the writing of a man whom Professor Dugald Stewart described from personal observation as talking like that, and of whom the Principal of Edinburgh University said that his conversation excelled his prose compositions. These also were in standard English, so that it is not surprising that so much of his best poetry is also. Yet certain modern writers (men of letters, not historians) have suggested that what was in fact his native tongue was an 'alien medium', to use Maurice Lindsay's term. When he wrote well in it, he was mastering 'what was essentially a foreign convention'. It is part of the thesis that the vernacular of Ayrshire

was the National Language of the whole of Scotland in a century in which Gaelic was the actual language of over half of the land mass.

Friar's Carse, whose laird and his lady presumably spoke English as correctly as the bard and their other guests, provided Burns with the masculine society in which he delighted, on a higher social and intellectual level than he had enjoyed in his earlier years. He repaid his debt to Captain Riddell by acting at his request as general organiser of the Monkland Friendly Society. 'Mr Burns,' wrote Riddell, 'was so good as to take the whole charge of this small concern. He was treasurer, librarian and censor to this little society, who will long have a grateful sense of his public spirit and exertions for their improvement and information.'

The society was designed to provide members of this rural community with good books to read, so that Burns was in effect a pioneer of the subscription library half a century before such institutions became the norm throughout Britain. But like so many would-be improvers of their fellow men, Burns found to his disappointment that many of his subscribers preferred 'damned trash' to the classics he wished to provide for them.

He was becoming increasingly interested in politics. On the centenary of the Glorious Revolution of 1688 which had deprived the last Stewart king of his throne and settled a Protestant Succession on his nephew and son-in-law William of Orange, Burns was moved to write on the subject to the *Edinburgh Evening Courant*. He could hardly have felt inclined to defend the cause of a Catholic autocrat who believed in the divine right of kings against one chosen by the will of the people expressed by an Act of Parliament, in those terms. But patriotic sentiment enlisted his sympathy on behalf of Scotland's last native dynasty, and a remarkably sound sense of history led him to protest against judging people of the past according to the standards and values of a later age.

In writing as he did, Burns was reacting to the sermon of a bigoted clergyman, and on another occasion he used one of his sharpest weapons, satire, in defence of the liberal Minister of Ayr, Dr William McGill, when he was attacked by his more intolerant colleagues for a theological tract that he had published.

> Doctor Mac, Doctor Mac, ye should [streek] on a
>   rack,   [stretch]
> To strike Evildoers with terror;
> To join FAITH and SENSE upon any pretence
> Was heretic, damnable error.
>
> *The Kirk of Scotland's Garland –*
> *a new Song.*

Such moderate Ministers as Dr McGill were often placed in their parishes through the patronage of the local lairds, a matter of controversy that John Galt described in his *Annals of the Parish*. In another poem Burns parodied the doggerel of the metrical psalms in his verses of thanksgiving for George III's recovery

---

Tam o' Shanter pursued by the witches.
Ah, Tam! Ah, Tam! Thou'll get thy fairin!
In hell they'll roast thee like a herrin!
In vain they Kate awaits thy comin!
Kate soon will be a woefu' woman!
From The Illustrated London News, *Burns Centenary issue, 1759.*

from his first attack of insanity, praying the Lord to save the country also from the evils of patronage and Dr McGill.

> And now thou hast restored our State,
> Pity our kirk also,
> For she by tribulations
> Is now brought very low!
>
> Consume that High-Place, PATRONAGE,
> From off thine holy hill;
> And in thy fury burn the book
> Even of that man, McGill.
>
> Now hear our Prayer, accept our Song,
> And fight thy Chosen's battle:
> We seek but little, Lord, from thee,
> Thou kens we get as little.
>
> *A new Psalm for the Chapel of*
> *Kilmarnock, on the thanksgiving-*
> *day for his Majesty's recovery.*

It took Burns longer than it ought to have done to realise that as a government servant in the Excise he did not enjoy his former freedom to comment on matters of Church and State. Another arena in which he was to air his views with dangerous indiscretion was the theatre of Dumfries. Before 1790 strolling players used to perform in the assembly room of the George Hotel there, and Burns would ride the six miles to and from Ellisland even in the depths of winter to watch a performance. He expressed a desire from time to time to write a play himself on a historical theme, but it is doubtful whether he possessed the aptitude, even if he had found the time to master the secrets of stage-craft.

In 1790 the foundation stone was laid of the Theatre Royal in Dumfries, though it was not completed until 1792. It was saved from demolition and restored a few decades ago, and remains the oldest in Scotland today. Patrick Miller, Burns' landlord, and Robert Riddell were among those who backed the project; and the company manager John Williamson and his assistant George Sutherland are remembered with honour for the part they played in fostering Scottish drama here at a time when it was frowned on by so many members of the Church establishment. The theatre could seat over 500 people, and in it Burns was to find a novel forum for his opinions.

An early example of his support of theatricals in Dumfries is the prologue he composed for a benefit performance on New Year's Night in 1790, before the theatre was built.

> Is there no daring Bard will rise and tell
> How glorious Wallace stood, how hapless fell?
> Where are the Muses fled that should produce
> A *drama* worthy of the name of Bruce?
> How on *this* spot he first unsheathed the sword
> 'Gainst mighty England and her guilty Lord . . .
>
> *Scots Prologue, For Mrs Sutherland's*
> *Benefit Night.*

In fact the immediate victim of Bruce's sword (or rather, dagger) had been his rival the Red Comyn, whom he slew before the very altar of the Greyfriars church in Dumfries, after inviting him there for a parley from Comyn's castle of Dalswinton, now the property of Patrick Miller. This area was steeped in history and the bard's verses were a moving plea for a Scottish playwright to step forward and do justice to its themes as Shakespeare had done in England.

His own genius was of an entirely different order, and among all his multifarious activities during these years he was devoting it to the creation of his crowning achievement. He had met the editor of the *Scots Musical Museum* for the first time in April 1787, and since James Johnson published his initial volume in that same year there were no more than two of Burns' songs in it. But when the second volume appeared in the following year it contained forty of the bard's productions, and his own introduction to the work. Johnson had shewn the good sense to hand over the role of editor to him, more or less. A third volume followed in 1790, with over fifty songs contributed by

Burns to it and a second preface written by himself.

Much scrupulous scholarship has been devoted to an analysis of these songs, few of which he ever claimed as his own compositions. Sometimes he created a song from a mere snatch of chorus. In the case of *John Anderson my Jo* it can be seen that he transformed some rather indecent verses into a moving celebration of love and loyalty in old age.

> John Anderson my jo, John,
> We clamb the hill the gither;
> And mony a [canty] day, John,   [cheerful]
> We've had wi' ane anither:
> Now we maun totter down, John,
> And hand in hand we'll go;
> And sleep [the gither] at the foot,   [together]
> John Anderson my Jo.

It is not merely that Burns rescued and improved, where so many 'improvers' of folk material have destroyed the essential quality of it, if not worse. Burns also possessed an unerring gift for matching words to melodies, which he would catch out of the air and sing over and over to himself, sometimes altering their speed to match them perfectly to the words with which he joined them in a lasting marriage.

We can follow his social diversions and bread-winning tasks during his residence at Ellisland. It is harder to follow him when he slipped away, often

---

Room in the Globe Tavern, Dumfries, from where Burns wrote to Graham of Fintry: 'I am going to give up, or sublet my farm directly.' From The Illustrated London News, *Burns Centenary issue, 1859.*

Drawing of house No 14 Caltonhill, Edinburgh the upper flat of which was the residence of M^{rs} McLehose — the "Clarinda" of Burns — and in which she died on the Morning of 22 October 1841

Above: Mrs Agnes M'Lehose (1759–1841), the grass widow whom Burns addressed as Clarinda and attempted without success to seduce: and her house at 14 Calton Hill, Edinburgh.

Below: Ellisland, the farm beside the River Nith in Dumfriesshire to which Burns moved after his marriage to Jean Armour. Engraving by R. Wilson from a drawing by J. O. Brown. Reproduced by courtesy of Mr Tom McIlwraith.

Dumfries today. The town stands about seven miles from the estuary of the River Nith. Burns knew the town well – the farm at Ellisland was six and a half miles away on the banks of the same river – and he was made an Honorary Burgess in 1787. He went to live there in November 1791 and died there in July 1796. The picture shows the Old Bridge, which dates from the 14th century, and the 'Caul' on the River Nith.

perhaps to that gazebo in the grounds of Friar's Carse, to concentrate on the work that has fixed him in immortal memory. This is the hidden factor, in assessing his decision, within a year of taking up his Excise duties, that he could not continue to combine these with farming as his predecessor Leonard Smith had done. He was also clear in his mind as to which job he should abandon. From the Globe Inn in Dumfries he wrote to Graham of Fintry on 4 September 1790: 'I am going to give up, or sublet my farm directly. . . Farming this place in which I live would just be a livelihood to a man who would be the greatest drudge in his own family, so is no object; and living here hinders me from that knowledge in the business of Excise which it is absolutely necessary for me to attain.'

By giving notice to his landlord of his desire to quit within three years of taking up his tenancy, Burns evaded the rise in rent to which he would have become liable at the end of that period. After describing Patrick Miller initially as 'my generous friend', he had spoken harshly of him when Ellisland proved less of a bargain than he had hoped. But Miller evidently gave him no further cause for complaint, although it took the bard a full year from the date of his letter of intent to Graham before he was rid of his farm. During that time his family was enlarged. A son had been added to it in August 1789, whom he named Francis Wallace in honour of Mrs Dunlop. In January 1791 his wife Jean

Clarinda in silhouette, by John Miers, c. 1790. Burns immortalized Agnes M'Lehose in the song:
Ae fond kiss, and then we sever;
Ae fareweel, and then for ever!
Scottish National Portrait Gallery, Edinburgh.

bore him another son, named William Nicol after the Latin teacher in Edinburgh who had accompanied him on his highland tour, and at almost the same time Anne Park bore him a daughter.

That summer Patrick Miller's own problem, how to dispose of Ellisland, was solved when the owner of an adjoining estate offered a price for it which Miller accepted. At this time Burns went off to Ayrshire to attend his brother Gilbert's wedding, and on his return he sold his crops by auction at a favourable price towards the end of August. In the following month he was released from his tenancy.

His affairs now in order, Burns paid his customary visit to Mrs Dunlop and, more surprisingly, another to Clarinda in Edinburgh. In November 1791 she wrote to him after a long silence, reminding him in formal terms of his obligations to Jenny Clow, the servant who had borne him a son, 'Your old acquaintance Jenny Clow who, to all appearance, is at the moment dying,' she remarked spitefully. Burns replied that he had offered to take the child into his care long ago 'but she would never consent'. He asked Clarinda to give her some money until he should come to Edinburgh to attend to the matter: and so the relationship had been restored to friendly terms by the time he encountered Clarinda, now 'my dearest Nancy' after their long separation. Poor Jenny had served her turn twice over.

Agnes M'Lehose had arranged to join her husband in Jamaica by the time she and Burns met in Edinburgh for the last time on 6 December. Forty years later she was to enter in her journal under that date: 'Parted with Burns, in the year 1791, never more to meet in this world. Oh, may we meet in Heaven.' For his part the bard commemorated their parting in a beautiful song which, as in the case of his address to Mary Campbell in heaven, gives little inkling of the real nature of their relationship. This is not to say that it is insincere, merely that the bard could perhaps write about love all the better because he had never experienced the actual emotion of being in love.

> Had we never loved sae kindly,
> Had we never loved sae blindly!
> Never met – or never parted,
> We had ne'er been brokenhearted.
>
> Ae fond kiss, and then we sever!
> Ae fareweel, Alas, for ever!
> Deep in heart-wrung tears I'll pledge thee,
> Warring sighs and groans I'll wage thee.
>
> *Song*, to the tune,
> *Rory Dall's port.*

By the time Burns unburdened his feelings in these terms he had already met another married woman, compared to whom Clarinda was now the farthing taper.

Robert Riddell possessed a younger brother named Walter like their father, who had gone to seek his fortune in the West Indies and found it when he

Mossgiel. Watercolour by J. Kennedy.

married the heiress of a sugar plantation in Antigua. Left a widower with this endowment, Walter Riddell next married the eighteen-year-old Maria Woodley, who had travelled out two years earlier to stay with her father, the Governor of the Leeward Islands. In the following year, 1791, Walter brought his young bride home and purchased an estate near to that of his elder brother which he named in his wife's honour Woodley Park.

He had brought to the doorstep of Burns the most intelligent girl with whom the bard ever formed a friendship, and the only one who was English. Connected on her mother's side with the nobility, the youthful author of a book about her West Indian travels that was well received and of poetry of more than average competence, Maria might easily have become bored with the conventional society of the Dumfriesshire gentry – and she was far from conventional herself. It is likely that she found particularly little to talk about with her sister-in-law from Manchester. But there was Burns, as magnetic a lodestone to her as she to him. Maria Riddell was the ultimate, the richest gift the bard received at Friar's Carse when he was introduced to her there.

Burns had taken his wife and family back to Mauchline at the time of the sale of Ellisland. In November 1791 they were installed in their new home in Dumfries.

Above: Friar's Carse, the property of Captain Robert Riddell, who gave Burns the key to the Hermitage in its grounds where tha bard could enjoy privacy. Watercolour by an unknown artist.

Below: Tam o'Shanter witnessing the revels of the witches in Alloway Kirk. Wash drawing by Alexander Carse, c. 1800.

*The estuary of the River Nith on the Solway Firth, the scene of
the poet's adventure in 1792 when, as an Exciseman, he led the
party which captured a smuggling vessel.*

Chapter 6

Ghost of Maecenas! hide thy blushing face!
They snatch'd him from the sickle and the plough –
To gauge ale-firkins.

To a Friend [Charles Lamb], *who*
had declared his intention of
writing no more poetry.

SAMUEL TAYLOR COLERIDGE, thirteen years younger than Burns, hailed him at his death as 'Nature's own beloved bard', and in these lines he invoked the generous Roman patron of letters, Maecenas, suggesting that Burns had lacked such patrons. In fact he enjoyed lavish patronage, of which he made the fullest use when it suited him, though he could treat those who were eager to assist him with scant courtesy when the spirit of independence moved him. Coleridge also implied that Burns was driven from his dignified, independent peasant life to one of drudgery in a demeaning profession.

This is equally far from the truth. 'Robert Burns Gentleman' of the Excise had employed farm labourers to handle his sickle and plough. He abandoned his occupation as a tenant farmer because he found his new one congenial, while his employers reported that he discharged his new duties with admirable efficiency. Had he lived, he might well have risen to a life of comparative leisure with the colossal salary of £1000

Dumfries Market Place. From Allan Cunningham: Pictures and Portraits of the Life and Land of Robert Burns, *1840.*

John Syme (1755–1831), who became Burns's closest friend in Dumfries. From the engraving by J. T. Kelly, c. 1800. Scottish National Portrait Gallery, Edinburgh.

a year, and he knew it. What he could not know was that, at the age of thirty-two, he was already a dying man.

The family moved into the middle floor of a house in what is now Bank Street, as tenants of Captain John Hamilton. It consisted of three rooms, each with a window facing the street, which ran down to the river Nith, the home of a blacksmith on the flat above and the Stamp Office of John Syme on the ground floor below. A stone spiral staircase ran up beside it. Here came Jean, now 26 years old, with her three sons Robert, aged 6, Francis aged 3 and the baby William. It was the first time Burns had made his home in comparatively cramped urban surroundings, and initially both he and his wife seem to have found it a strain. 'My wife scolds me, my business torments me, and my sins come staring me in the face,' he complained a fortnight after he had moved in. Another winter was laying its hold on his sick heart. But in Dumfries he was transferred to an Excise district

within the town, where he could make his rounds on foot, instead of being required to undertake those arduous journeys on horseback.

We can still see his first home there, through the perseverance of James Urquhart, the local historian. At a time when the Town Council was considering the demolition of this tenement to provide a site for public toilets, he purchased its derelict upper storeys, in which the Burns family had lived, and preserved them from destruction until Mr and Mrs Robert Laird stepped forward with an undertaking to renovate the property as their home. The work was completed in 1981, ensuring that the outer fabric at least will remain very much as the bard knew it.

His discontent in his new surroundings was soon eased by his acquaintance with John Syme in the office below, who was to become his closest friend in Dumfries. Syme was the son of a Kirkcudbright laird, a few years older than the bard, another member of the gentry with whom he consorted so amicably despite his

Above: Mrs Maria Riddell (1772–1808), from the portrait by Sir Thomas Lawrence. The most intelligent and understanding woman with whom Burns ever formed a friendship. National Trust, Kingston Lacy, Dorset.

Opposite: The statue of King Robert Bruce at Bannockburn. Burns placed in his mouth the most stirring of his patriotic songs: 'Scots, wha hae wi' Wallace bled. . .'

strictures on their class. Syme, for his part, left his own graphic portrait of his new neighbour.

'The poet's expression varied perpetually, according to the idea that predominated in his mind; and it was beautiful to remark how well the play of his lips indicated the sentiment he was about to utter. His eyes and lips – the first remarkable for fire, and the second for flexibility – formed at all times an index to his mind, and, as sunshine or shade predominated, you might have been told, *a priori*, whether the company was to be favoured with a scintillation of wit, or a sentiment of benevolence, or a burst of fiery indignation.'

By the time John Syme wrote that, Scott had already published his description of the eyes which 'glowed, I say literally *glowed*,' recalling his meeting with Burns in Edinburgh when he was a youth. 'I cordially concur with what Sir Walter Scott says of the poet's eyes,' wrote Syme. 'In animated moments, and particularly when his anger was aroused by instances of tergiversation, meanness, or tyranny, they were actually like coals of living fire.'

The two men shared advanced liberal opinions, and so did another professional man with whom Burns developed a warm acquaintance in Dumfries, the physician William Maxwell. He was a year younger than the bard, and had served as a doctor with the Republican forces in France during the revolution there; he was at the scaffold when Louis XIV was excuted. The views of such men were not confined to any particular rank of society in Scotland at this time. The Earl of Buchan's son Henry Erskine, who had patronized Burns in Edinburgh and who rose to the position of Lord Advocate, was a lifelong liberal. Lord Daer, the Earl of Selkirk's heir, was as outspoken a supporter of constitutional reform as Syme, Maxwell or Burns. A few years later the Earl of Dundonald's heir, Lord Cochrane, proved a more active radical than any of them.

But once the bard had become a government servant, it behoved him to be discreet in his political statements, and particularly in his comments on the French revolution at a time when Britain was moving towards war with France. Ever forthright to the point of tactlessness in his expressions of opinion, it took him longer than it ought to have done to appreciate this.

In the circumstances he was extraordinarily fortunate in his immediate superior in the Excise. Alexander Findlater was a man of the utmost integrity, and Burns discovered how punctilious he was in his supervision in June 1791 when Findlater questioned one of the entries in his books. It concerned a local farmer named William Lorimer. No doubt as many people attempted tax evasion then as now, and Lorimer's subterfuges are revealed in the letter Burns wrote, explaining what had occurred. Evidently the farmer had been concealing part of his stock from scrutiny.

'The last survey I made prior to Mr Lorimer's going to Edinburgh I was very particular in my inspection and the quantity was certainly in his possession as I stated it. The surveys I have made during his absence might as well have been marked "key absent" as I never found any body but the lady, who I know is not mistress of the keys., &c. to know anything of it, and one of the times it would have rejoiced all Hell to have seen her so drunk . . .' Burns was anxious to retain his reputation for efficiency, as indeed he did.

'I know, Sir, and regret deeply that this business glances with a malign aspect on my character as an Officer; but as I am really innocent in the affair, and as this gentleman is known to be an illicit dealer, and particularly as this is the *single* instance of the least shadow of carelessness or impropriety in my conduct as an Officer, I shall be peculiarly unfortunate if my character shall fall a sacrifice to the dark manoevres of a Smuggler.' The postscript to this letter strikes an altogether different note. 'I send you some rhymes I have just finished which tickle my fancy a little.' Findlater's subordinate might go over his head to higher authority: he might compromise the service by his seditious utterances. But even if he had proved careless on more than this one occasion the association would still have been the privilege of a lifetime, and it is clear that Findlater knew it.

His own superior John Mitchell was equally appreciative, just as tolerant when the bard used his social connections to intrigue with higher authority behind his back, no less loyal when Burns found himself in trouble. Mitchell's friendship and hospitality to the bard was rewarded, soon after his move to Dumfries, with the much-sung song:

> The deil cam fiddlin thro' the town,
> And danc'd awa wi' th' Exciseman;
> And ilka wife cries, auld [Mahoun],   [Devil]
> I wish you luck o' the prize, man.
>
> *The De'il's awa wi' th' Exciseman.*

As for Burns' relationship with the Lorimers, who had lived only two miles away from him at Ellisland, there is no means of telling how it was complicated (if at all) by his fondness for their daughter Jean. It would have been extremely odd if he had not 'tried for intimacy', though several of the poems he addressed to her suggest that he was unsuccessful, quite apart from the fact that she did not become pregnant, the almost inevitable result of the bard's conquests. He gave her a pseudonym, and presented a copy of his poems to her with the inscription: 'To the Lady whom in so many fictitious reveries of Passion but with the most ardent sentiments of *real* friendship, I have so often sung under the name of CHLORIS.'

Most precious of all to Burns according to his own submission was the society of Friar's Carse, and especially after the arrival there of Maria Riddell. He wrote a revealing comment on her to the Edinburgh printer William Smellie, who had introduced him to the Crochallan Fencibles, in January 1792. She wished to consult him about her book of travels, and Burns

Jean Lorimer (Chloris) (1775–1831), daughter of Burns's neighbour at Ellisland. From a portrait miniature by an unknown artist. National Gallery of Scotland.

warned him: 'the Lady has one unlucky failing; a failing which you will easily discover, as she seems rather pleased with indulging it; and a failing which you will easily pardon, as it is a sin that very much besets yourself: where she dislikes or despises, she is apt to make no more a secret of it – than where she esteems and respects'. That was something else they had in common.

In the following month Burns was promoted to the Port Division of the Excise, in a post that carried a salary of £70 a year, double that of a Minister of the Gospel, with handsome perquisites. In the very month of his promotion a vessel manned by smugglers was reported in the Solway Firth, into which the river Nith flows, a few miles south of Dumfries. A Revenue Officer, Walter Crawford, sent his colleague John Lewars to the town to call out members of the 3rd Regiment of Dragoons who were stationed there at the time. They attacked the ship, by now marooned on a mud bank, in three parties, one of them led by Burns. He waded breast-high through the water and was first aboard, while the crew fled across the sands to the English shore. The vessel and her contents were sold in Dumfries, and Burns must have received his share of the prize money. Such incidents were not rare. The mast of a smuggling vessel captured in Burns's time was converted to the use of a centre-post in a local wind-mill, and is now to be seen in the spiral staircase of Dumfries Burgh Museum.

It cannot have improved Burns' health to wade in the waters of the Solway Firth in winter, but in general his new job was lighter, as well as better paid. Instead of having to ride for hundreds of miles each week, he could now walk everywhere in the discharge of his duties. He had written earlier: 'Here I sit, altogether Novemberish, a damned melange of Fretfulness and

Robert Burns. The portrait by Alexander Naysmith, 1787.

Opposite: Robert Burns. The statue at Dumfries.

Melancholy; not enough of the one to rouse me to passion, nor of the other to repose me in torpor.' He must have learned to dread the onset of each winter, but his promotion to the Port Division promised a measure of relief in the future.

In September 1792 the new Theatre Royal opened, and now Burns lived so close to it he could enjoy the pleasures of the stage without having to ride for miles from Ellisland. Shakespeare's *As You Like It* was performed in October, and he was present when there was a disturbance during the playing of the National Anthem. It appears that he remained seated instead of standing in honour of the King, while some called for the revolutionary French song 'Ça Ira' with its threat to kill aristocrats. Only a few weeks later Burns contributed an address to be declaimed by the actress who played *The Country Girl*, containing an indiscreet reference to Thomas Paine's *The Rights of Man*. Paine was a former Exciseman, who had fled to France in this very year to escape criminal proceedings – where he narrowly escaped being guillotined by Robespierre.

Robert Burns ought not to have been surprised when he learned that his conduct was to be investigated, but he was. As usual, he appealed over the heads of his superiors, Findlater and Mitchell, in a grovelling letter to Graham of Fintry.

'I have been surprised, confounded and distracted by Mr Mitchell, the Collector, telling me just now, that he has received an order from your Honourable Board to enquire into my political conduct, and blaming me as a person disaffected to Government. Sir, you are a Husband – and a father – you know what you would feel, to see the much-loved wife of your bosom, and your helpless, prattling little ones, turned adrift into the world, degraded and disgraced from a situation in which they have been respectable and respected, and left almost without the necessary support of a miserable existence. Alas, Sir! must I think that such, soon, will be my lot! And from the damned, dark insinuations of hellish vile, groundless Envy too!' This kind of crescendo, working up to a dramatic climax, had been a recurrent feature in the correspondence of Burns for many years, whenever his feelings were aroused.

Graham replied in the New Year of 1793, kindly informing him of the evidence that had been brought against him. This prompted Burns to describe what had occurred at the Theatre Royal. 'I was in the playhouse one night, when ÇA IRA was called for. I was in the middle of the Pit, and from the Pit the clamour arose. One or two individuals with whom I occasionally associate were of the party, but I neither knew of the Plot, nor joined in the Plot; nor ever opened my lips to hiss or huzza, that, or any other Political tune whatever.'

It sounds a little disingenuous, and so do his protestations of loyalty to the royal family whom he had described so offensively in the verse he scratched on the window in Stirling with the diamond given to him by the Earl of Glencairn. 'I always revered, and ever will,

with the soundest loyalty, revere, the monarch of Great Britain as, to speak in Masonic, the sacred KEYSTONE OF OUR ROYAL ARCH CONSTITUTION.' In Dumfries his Masonic connections remained as close as ever, though the measure of protection this gave him can only be guessed.

Perhaps his superiors in the Excise intended only to teach him a timely lesson by giving him a fright. Certainly the apostle of the underdog was sustained as usual by sympathy in high places. John Erskine, a scion of the Earls of Mar, made contact with Robert Riddell as soon as he heard of the bard's difficulties, enquiring whether a fund might be raised for his relief. But the fracas was soon 'set to rights', as Burns was able to inform Mrs Dunlop, while he did not even wait to hear that his name had been cleared before asking Graham whether he might replace the Supervisor of the Excise District of Galloway, who was ill.

It was William Nicol the Latin teacher who gave his friend the most sensible advice. Referring to George III's recurrent insanity, he wrote: 'Dear Christless Bobby, What concerns it thee whether the lousy Dumfriesian fiddlers play "Ça ira" or "God save the King?" Suppose you *had* an aversion to the King, you could not, as a gentleman, wish God to use him worse than He has done.'

God was not using Burns much better. That winter he was stricken again with the symptoms of his heart disease. Yet his mind remained as active as ever, and it took an interesting turn in the letter of appreciation he wrote to John Erskine after Robert Riddell had shewn him Erskine's proposal for the bard's relief. He referred to his 'humble station', which was not unreasonable in the relative scale of things when addressing a descendant of Earls. But he distanced himself from 'the uninformed mob', identifying himself with the middle class.

'Does any man tell me, that my feeble efforts can be of no service; and that it does not belong to my humble station to meddle with the concerns of a People? I tell him, that it is on such individuals as I, that for the hand of support and the eye of intelligence, a Nation has to rest. The uninformed mob may swell a nation's bulk; and the titled, tinsel Courtly throng may be its feathered ornament, but the number of those who are elevated enough in life, to reason and reflect; and yet low enough to keep clear of the real contagion of a Court; these are a Nation's strength.'

Burns may or may not have been trimming his thoughts to the aristocrat he was addressing, yet he was more disrespectful still of the lower orders in a letter he wrote to William Niven, recipient of the earliest of all that have survived, dating back to 1780. 'Never blow my songs among the million,' he told Niven in Kirkoswald, 'as I would abhor to hear every Prentice mouthing my poor performances in the streets.' Yet when the parish Minister compiled his entry for the *Statistical Account of Scotland* and failed to mention the Monkland Friendly Society, Robert

Burns contributed a note on the subject, signing himself 'A Peasant'. Pathologically class-conscious as he was, he was also a natural actor who loved to appear in different costumes. The spectrum of language in his poetry reveals the same chameleon quality.

He was intensely self-conscious about this. In August 1793 he wrote, 'I have not that command of the [English] language that I have of my native tongue. In fact, I think my ideas are more barren in English than in Scottish.' People think in the language in which they speak and express themselves in their letters, and several sound judges remarked that Burns was most brilliantly expressive in his conversation and in his correspondence. After having bewitched so many audiences by his talk in what was described as standard English, and written so many hundreds of letters that he could perfectly well have composed in his 'native tongue' if he had chosen to do so, it was rather late in the day to pretend that he lacked command of the language. But he was writing those words to a man who had never met him, and to whom he could safely strike any attitude he chose.

His name was George Thomson, the son of a Fife school teacher who had been educated in north-east Scotland, and was now emulating James Johnson in collecting folk songs for publication. Naturally these were in various dialects, depending on what part of the country they derived from. Of course the words were in Gaelic throughout the greater part of the rural areas, their dialects similarly varied. The Lowland collectors

George Thomson (1757–1851), the collector of folk-songs to whom Burns wrote such revealing letters about his methods of work. Anonymous portrait, based on the painting by Sir Henry Raeburn. Scottish National Portrait Gallery, Edinburgh.

sixth bar of the second Part, the place where these three syllables will always recur, that the four semiquavers usually sung as one syllable, will with the greatest propriety divide into two as thus:

For nature made her what she is, and &c. &c. &c.

I have hitherto deferred the sublimer, more pathetic airs, untill more leisure, as they will take & deserve, a greater effort. However, they are all put into thy hands, as clay into the hands of the Potter; to make one vessel to honor, & another to dishonor. —— Farewel.

Robt. Burns

knew nothing of this, and harvested only the melodies from this fruitful source. Many of the Gaelic songs had Jacobite themes, which Burns himself used on more than one occasion. 'It was a' for our rightfu' king' is considered to be his best Jacobite song, and certainly it can stand comparison with the best that the Gaels composed for themselves on this subject.

George Thomson wrote to Burns in September 1792, only a week or two before the Theatre Royal opened for the first time, enlisting his support in his new enterprise. 'For some years past, I have, with a friend or two, employed many leisure hours in collating and collecting the most favourite of our national melodies, for publication . . . To render this work perfect, we are desirous to have the poetry improved wherever it seems unworthy of the music.' He offered to pay 'any reasonable price you shall please to demand'.

Burns accepted the invitation but refused the fee. 'As to any remuneration, you may think my Songs either *above* or *below* price; for they shall absolutely be the one or the other. In the honest enthusiasm with which I embark in your undertaking, to talk of money, wages, fee, for hire, &c. could be downright Sodomy of Soul!'

1792 was the year in which the fourth volume of Johnson's *Scots Museum* was published, about half of its songs contributed by Burns, and still he continued to send others for a fifth. Now he began to feed Thomson as well, while Creech in Edinburgh brought out a new edition of his poems in February 1793, enlarged by the inclusion of *Tam o' Shanter* among other pieces. Recovering both from his sickness and from the fright he had been given by his superiors in the Excise, he had much to occupy and hearten him as spring approached.

When Thomson's *A Select Collection of Original Scottish Airs* was published in June he sent the bard five pounds as a token of his gratitude. Burns' response exhibits him at his most churlish. Instead of either accepting it graciously or refusing it with dignity, he responded: 'I assure you, my dear Sir, that you truly hurt me with your pecuniary parcel. It degrades me in my own eyes. However, to return it would savour of bombast affectation.' And more to the same effect, ending with the flourish: 'BURNS'S character for Generosity of Sentiment, and Independence of Mind, will, I trust, long outlive any of his wants which the cold, unfeeling, dirty Ore can supply: at least, I shall take care that such a Character he shall deserve.' William Creech had been too mean to offer Burns any payment for his new edition, and thus protected himself against such a snub.

George Thomson was to prove a far less satisfactory colleague than Johnson. He altered the bard's poems without his permission, and failed to return material that he did not choose to publish himself, lest it should be passed to his rival. Yet he performed an inestimable service by provoking Burns into writing long, revealing explanations of his methods of work. One of these tells how he came to compose his most patriotic song, *Scots, wha hae wi' Wallace bled*, in 1793 to an air that he had used as early as 1788 for a drinking song.

'I am delighted with many little melodies, which the learned musician despises as silly and insipid. I do not know whether the old air "Hey, tutti, taitie" may rank among this number; but well I know that . . . it has often filled my eyes with tears. There is a tradition, which I have met with in many places of Scotland, that it was Robert Bruce's March at the battle of Bannockburn. This thought, in my yesternight's evening walk, warmed me to a pitch of enthusiasm on the theme of Liberty and Independence, which I threw into a kind of Scots Ode, fitted to the Air, that one might suppose to be the gallant ROYAL SCOT'S address to his heroic followers on that eventful morning.' While the poetry of his last years brought him no addition to his professional salary, Burns was stimulated by the demand for his songs, by the sense of achievement that is dearest to every author, and (although he was ever the soundest judge of his own work) by his public recognition.

In May Burns moved with his family from Bank Street to what is now named Burns Street. His daughter Elizabeth had been born in the previous November and he required larger accommodation, which the same Captain Hamilton provided, whose tenant he had been in his previous home. The one in which he ended his life has been preserved as a museum, so that its interior can be examined, almost exactly as it was when the bard lived there. As his first winter approached in these more ample surroundings, he wrote an ominous letter to his old friend Robert Cleghorn of the Crochallan Fencibles.

'From my late hours last night, and the dripping fogs and damned east-wind of this stupid day, I have left me as little soul as an oyster. "Sir John, you are so fretful, you cannot live long." "Why, there is it! Come, sing me a BAUDY-SONG to make me merry!!!"' He enclosed one of his own.

> In Edinburgh town they've made a law,
> In Edinburgh at the Court o' Session,
> That standing pricks are fautors a'
> And guilty of a high transgression.
>
> *Act Sederunt of the Session – A Scots Ballad*, to the tune, *O'er the muir amang the heather.*

As for his late hours the night before, such scraps of evidence were used by his first biographer, Dr James Currie, to suggest that Burns was dying of alcoholism. Currie was a teetotaller who, like other physicians,

knew nothing of endocarditis. He was refuted by the man whose evidence on the subject can be taken as final, the bard's professional superior, Alexander Findlater. 'The superintendence of his behaviour was my special province,' he deposed. 'I never beheld anything like the gross enormities with which he is now charged.' The writings of Burns also contradict the charge. They reveal that he retained his clarity of mind unimpaired until the moment of his death, as those who die of alcoholic poisoning never do.

But as his health became more precarious, late nights and even moderate doses of drink could affect his nervous system and influence his behaviour, and this was what brought his happy association with Friar's Carse to an abrupt end, during the winter of 1793. Maria Riddell's husband had returned to the West Indies, in an attempt to raise the remainder of the purchase price of Woodley Park, and it is highly probable, though not certain, that she was among the guests with Robert Burns on the fatal evening. As a rule he did not remain for long drinking with the men, after dinner, but left them to join the ladies. But on this occasion he delayed while his male companions amused themselves by discussing the rape of the Sabine women by the Romans. In their cups they decided to re-enact the episode.

Burns, by his own admission, was not over-delicate in his physical approaches to the opposite sex, and even if he did not 'try for intimacy' with customary directness, he certainly caused grave offence. This would not have been difficult when the target selected for him was Mrs Robert Riddell, a prim woman with whom he had failed to establish warm relations in more conventional circumstances. Whatever he did, he was expelled from the house. The letter of apology he sent to his hostess may be interpreted variously. It works up to a hysterical climax in characteristic fashion, but it also contains an element of hyperbole which suggests

that he was writing tongue in cheek, failing to understand the gravity of the situation.

'I daresay that this is the first epistle you ever received from this nether world,' he told Mrs Riddell. 'I write you from the regions of Hell, amid the horrors of the damned. The time and manner of my leaving your hearth I do not exactly know, as I took my departure in the heat of a fever of intoxication, contracted at your hospitable mansion; but on my arrival here, I was fairly tried, and sentenced to endure the purgatorial tortures of this infernal confine for the space of ninety-nine years, eleven months, and twenty-nine days, and all on account of the impropriety of my conduct yesternight under your roof.'

He blamed his associates as he probably had every right to do. They may well have incited him, as a joke. 'To the men of the company I will make no apology. Your husband, who insisted on my drinking more than I chose, has no right to blame me; and the other gentlemen were partakers of my guilt. But to you, Madam, I have much to apologise. Your good opinion I valued as one of the greatest acquisitions I had made on earth, and I was truly a beast to forfeit it.'

So he moved towards his peroration. 'Regret! Remorse! Shame! ye three hellhounds that ever dog my steps and bay at my heels, spare me! spare me! Forgive the offences, and pity the perdition of, Madam, Your humble servant.' She did not, and her husband Robert Riddell, who would surely have done so, died suddenly a few months later. The doors of Friar's Carse had closed on Robert Burns forever.

The member of the family on whom he rounded in his anger was Maria, over ten years younger than himself, his delightful, understanding admirer. Propriety compelled her to support her outraged sister-in-law, whether or not she had been present on the Sabine evening, or shared the views of other ladies who witnessed the scene. In any case she could not invite the bard to Woodley Park while her husband was still in the West Indies. Scurrilous as he could be, particularly about women, Burns made her the target for some of his most contemptible verses. His *Monody on Maria* ends with the epitaph:

> Here lies, now a prey to insulting Neglect,
> What once was a butterfly gay in life's beam:
> Want only of wisdom denied her respect,
> Want only of goodness denied her esteem.

He excelled even that in the verses he pinned to her carriage in public.

> If you rattle along like your Mistress's tongue,
> Your speed will outrival the dart:
> But, a fly for your load, you'll break down on the
>   road,
> If your stuff be as rotten's her heart.

The most that can be said in his favour is that by 1794 his own sick heart was undermining the magnanimity of soul which always triumphed, sooner or later, over his irascible nature. He wrote in February, as usual in the rigours of winter, 'For these two months I have not been able to lift a pen. My constitution and frame were, ab origine, blasted with a deep taint of hypochondria, which poisons my existence.' To add to the problems of his own health, there were those of his little daughter Elizabeth, whose young life was already fading to its close.

But he rallied as the spring came, for the last time, and in June he went on a six-day tour to the south-west in the company of John Syme, riding a Highland pony. They spent three days at Kenmure Castle, the home of the Jacobite Earl of Kenmure, who had taken part in the 1715 uprising. Then they visited the Earl of Selkirk at St. Mary's Isle where the Italian composer Pietro Urbani was among the guests. 'Urbani,' wrote Syme, 'sung us some Scotch songs accompanied with music. The two young ladies of Selkirk sung also. We had the song "Lord Gregory" which I asked for, to have occasion to call upon Burns to speak his words to that tune.' The Earl's daughter Lady Mary Douglas lent the bard her copy of *Orpheus Caledonius*; while he composed the Selkirk grace:

> Some have meat and cannot eat,
> Some can not eat that want it:
> But we have meat and we can eat,
> Sae let the Lord be thankit.

By a strange chance it was the bard's superior Alexander Findlater who fell ill in the winter of 1794 rather than himself, so that he became acting Supervisor of the Excise division of Dumfries. Beyond this post lay the comparatively idle office of Collector which, as he mentioned to his former landlord Patrick Miller, could earn him upwards of £1000 a year. To cheer him further, the generous Maria responded to his first overture in 1795. He was able to tell her that Alexander Reid had made a miniature portrait of him in ivory: 'I think he has hit by far the best likeness of me ever taken.' Others have decided that it is the only true likeness of him in existence.

What is so astonishing is that it could still depict the features that had cast such a magic spell; the penetrating look, strong jaw, square head and dominating air. He had been painted for the first time by Alexander Nasmyth in Edinburgh, who presented him as a well-born aesthete fresh from Eton and Oxford, and reproduced this portrait in an even more saintly version before wisely abandoning portraiture in favour of landscape. Still he could not leave Burns alone, but composed a posthumous, full-length picture of him, sturdily communing with nature in the countryside with features that bear no resemblance to his other interpretations. It is the Nasmyth portraits that have been reproduced by the million as true likenesses of Burns. As if by a superhuman effort, Burns preserved his physiognomy intact until Reid could record it better for posterity.

But he achieved this by only a narrow margin. That

Kenmure Castle. From Francis Grose: The Antiquities of Scotland, *1797. John Gordon, the 7th Viscount, entertained Burns and John Syme in July 1793. His grandfather, a Jacobite lord who lost his head in 1715, became the subject of Burns's* O Kenmure's on and awa, Willie.

winter Burns began to display an anxiety neurosis about money that was to accompany him to the grave. Certainly the French war had diminished his perquisites, while his family had been increased by the birth of James Glencairn in August 1784. But since his assets greatly exceeded his debts at his death, it is hard to resist a suspicion that his financial worries were at least partly symptoms of manic depression. He asked for a loan of three guineas in January 1785, and merely from an acquaintance, not from George Thomson whose payment he had scorned. A fortnight later he was apologising to his landlord because he was behind-hand with his rent, and Captain Hamilton was setting his mind at rest with an invitation to visit him. Yet he enlisted in the Dumfries Volunteers, until the additional exertion made him 'so ill as to be scarce able to hold this miserable pen to this miserable paper', as he told Maria in the spring. The ease of mind which her reconciliation brought to him was undone by his final rupture with Mrs. Dunlop of Dunlop.

The exact cause of it can only be surmised. She was an elderly, conventional woman who had written him over a hundred letters, that ought to have told him where the limits of her tolerance lay. She possessed a son in the army at a time when Britain was at war with republican France, and two French refugee sons in law. On 12 January 1795 Burns wrote to her describing the murdered King and Queen of France as a 'perjured Blockhead and unprincipled Prostitute', who deserved their fate. Some have doubted whether this could have sufficed to reduce her to such unforgiving silence, but no other explanation has ever been found.

Burns would have been kinder to himself in his last year of life if he had taken to his bed: he might also have preserved it for longer if he had given himself the rest that his tired heart needed. But instead he fought his disease with a courage that throws a retrospective light on all his previous actions, ever since he had slaved for his relentless father as a boy. He continued to send songs of the highest quality both to Johnson and to Thomson, and much that he wrote in these last months, both in prose and verse, might have made the angels weep.

His end was hastened by the course of treatment prescribed for him by his devoted friend Dr. William Maxwell. Paradoxically, Scotland at this time led the world in the field of scientific medicine. In the lifetime of Burns the first centre of clinical training was

*Brow on the Solway, where the dying bard drank the waters,
and waded daily in the sea. Engraving by D. O. Hill for Wilson
and Chambers,* The Land of Burns, *1840.*

established in America at Philadelphia, and it was designed and staffed entirely by Edinburgh graduates. But it was not until a few years after the death of Burns that Laennec invented the stethoscope, opening the path to a knowledge of heart disease.

The remedy Maxwell recommended for what he diagnosed as the bard's 'flying gout' was one that had long been fashionable in Scotland. At Peterhead there was a well beside which the Freemasons had built a Lodge in the year of Burns' birth, and here patients came to drink the water and also to bathe in the frigid sea water. There was another therapeutic spa at Moffat, but unluckily for Burns the nearest to Dumfries was Brow Well where patients could immerse themselves in the Solway as well as drink the water. Maxwell advised Burns to combine this treatment with energetic horseriding, but by the time he did so, his patient was too weak to mount a horse.

His pain and wretchedness seeped into his letters. In January 1796 he wrote to tell Mrs Dunlop of little Elizabeth's death. 'The Autumn robbed me of my only daughter & darling child . . . I had scarcely begun to recover from that shock when [I] became myself the victim of a most severe Rheumatic fever, and long the die spun doubtful; until after many weeks of a sick-bed it seems to have turned up more life, and I am beginning to crawl across my room, and once indeed have been before my own door in the street.' Still Mrs Dunlop did not reply.

At the end of April he told George Thomson: 'Almost ever since I wrote to you last, I have only known Existence by the pressure of the heavy hand of sickness; and have counted time by the repercussions of PAIN! Rheumatism, Cold and Fever have formed, to me, a terrible Trinity in Unity, which makes me close my eyes in misery, and open them without hope.' In a remarkable poem on life and death that he addressed to the Colonel of the Dumfries Volunteers he exclaimed (note that 'warld' requires two syllables here – 'warald'):

O what a [canty] warld were it,   [cheerful]
Would pain and care, and sickness spare it.

In June he wrote what proved to be his farewell letter to James Johnson, enquiring about the fifth volume of the *Scots Museum*. 'You may probably think that for some time past I have neglected you and your work; but, Alas, the hand of pain, and sorrow, and care has these many months lain heavy on me! Personal and domestic affliction have almost entirely banished that alacrity and life with which I used to woo the rural Muse of Scotia. In the meantime, let us finish what we have so well begun.'

On 3 July he dragged himself the nine miles to Brow

Well, where he drank the water, and waded daily, chest-deep in the muddy sea. Here he wrote his last letter to Mrs Dunlop.

'Madam, I have written you so often without receiving any answer, that I would not trouble you again but for the circumstances in which I am. An illness which has long hung about me in all probability will speedily send me beyond that bourne whence no traveller returns. Your friendship with which for many years you honoured me was a friendship dearest to my soul. Your conversation and especially your correspondence were at once highly entertaining and instructive. With what pleasure did I use to break up the seal! The remembrance yet adds one pulse more to my poor palpitating heart. Farewell!!!'

His farewell letter to his brother Gilbert contains his financial worries, which were illusory because his friends were poised to help in any way they could, and particularly his colleagues in the Excise. 'I have been a week at sea-bathing, and I will continue there or in a friend's house in the country all the summer. God help my wife and children, if I am taken from their head! They will be poor indeed. I have contracted one or two serious debts, partly from my illness these many months and partly from too much thoughtlessness as to expence when I came to town that will cut in too much on the little I leave them in your hands. Remember me to my Mother.'

The Dumfries Volunteers paid for their own uniforms, and Burns's state of mind may be judged by his reaction when he received the tailor's bill. He wrote to his cousin James Burness, the lawyer in Montrose: 'When you offered me money-assistance little did I think I should want it so soon. A rascal of a Haberdasher to whom I owe a considerable bill taking it into his head that I am dying, has commenced a process against me, and will infallibly put my emaciated body in jail. Will you be so good as to accommodate me, and that by return of post, with ten pound. O, James! did you know the pride of my heart, you would feel doubly for me! Alas! I am not used to beg!' His humiliation was doubled when he felt obliged to write to Thomson: 'After all my boasted independence, curst necessity compels me to implore you for five pounds.'

Maria Riddell had not seen Burns since he resembled the portrait of Alexander Reid. Before he went to Brow Well she had invited him to accompany her, in the uniform of the Dumfries Volunteers, to the Royal Birthday ball in Dumfries. 'I am in such miserable health,' he replied, 'as to be utterly incapable of shewing my loyalty in any way.' But still she did not realize what was in store for her when she sent her carriage to Brow Well on 7 July to bring him to their final meeting. As he stumbled out of it, he met her look of consternation with the question: 'Well Madam, and have you any commands for the next world?' He remained a magnificent actor to the last.

Mrs Riddell provided the final, conclusive testimony concerning the bard's state of mind on the threshold of death, proving that it was entirely unclouded by alcoholism. 'I had seldom seen his mind greater or more

The room in which Burns died on 21 July 1796. Anonymous wash drawing.

1817, one of her sons was a civil servant in London, while two others were advancing towards the rank of Colonel in the army. Mrs Burns felt able to decline the offer of assistance, a gesture worthy of such a husband as she had possessed.

By this time his remains had been removed from their original resting place, to the vault of a costly mausoleum, one of the many memorials and statues that were to be built by public subscription throughout the country. Books about his life and writings, provoked in the first instance by the libels of Dr Currie, have likewise proliferated all over the world. One of these, outstanding for its incisive brevity and its good sense, is *There was a Lad*, published in 1949 by Hilton Brown. It concludes with these words:

'Small wonder that Burns's story has intrigued not only his countrymen, but a great part of mankind; so that an American could say – with whatever hyperbole – that his name had been "dearer to a greater number of hearts than any other save that of Christ"; and a Chinese could find him revealing "our common humanity"; and a Canadian could write, "He made the world his lover". Whatever value may be attached to Burns's writings, verse or prose, whatever blame he may have earned by his faults and his failings, it is surely a poor heart that will not take fire at the warm blaze of his own and subscribe to the conclusion – "Here was a great *man*".'

Jean Armour, Mrs Robert Burns, in her 62nd year. Reproduced from a silhouette by W. Seville in the possession of Fred. Finlayson, Kirkcudbright.

Acknowledgements

BBC Hulton Picture Library 11, 29; City of Edinburgh District Council Museums & Galleries 44 top, 46/47, 78 top, 88, 122 top; W. F. Davidson 99, 103, 106, 111; by courtesy of Edinburgh City Libraries 13, 15, 28, 40, 44, 45, 76, 81, 91, 104, 117; H.G.P.L. 14 top, 20/21, 34, 43, 82 top, 90, 119; Jarrold Colour Publications 67 bottom, 70, 74 bottom, 98 bottom; The Mansell Collection 8, 9, 16 bottom, 23, 24, 32, 39, 42, 58 right, 69 bottom, 87 top, 97, 123; J. A. McCook, Photographer, Nethy Bridge 66 bottom; Mary Evans Picture Library 12 left, 31 top; Mitchell Library/Glasgow District Libraries 56, 73, 80, 81 centre, 81 bottom, 87 bottom, 114, 124; National Galleries of Scotland 12 right, 16 top, 17, 18, 21 top, 25, 31 bottom, 38, 50, 51 top, 51 bottom, 53, 55 bottom, 59, 60/61, 63, 64 bottom, 65, 66 top, 67 top, 69 top, 71 top, 71 bottom, 72, 74 top, 75, 77, 78 bottom, 79, 83, 84, 85 top, 85 bottom, 86, 92, 93 bottom, 96, 98 top, 100, 101, 102 bottom, 102 top, 109, 110, 113, 116, 121, 122; National Library of Scotland 14 bottom, 22 top, 22 bottom, 29 top, 35, 48, 55 top, 57, 58 left, 64 top, 68, 82 bottom, 105, 120; National Portrait Gallery, London 26, National Trust Photo Library 107; Scottish Tourist Board 19, 36.

Index

Page numbers in *italic* refer to captions